Dr Jean Coope studied at Manchester University, from where she graduated in 1951-2. She has been a general practitioner in her husband's practice near Macclesfield, England since 1953, at the same time working in a Family Planning (contraceptive) clinic.

Since 1972 she has undertaken research into the menopause and its treatments, especially hormone replacement therapy, and she has published many papers on the subject. In 1978 she became MRCGP (Manchester University) for her work on the menopause.

Dr Coope has six children and many interests outside her research work, particularly music and the opera.

D1349491

POSITIVE HEALTH GUIDE

THE
MENOPAUSE
Coping with the change

Dr Jean Coope,
MD, MRCGP, DObst, RCOG

Foreword by Prof Ian D. Cooke,
*Department of Obstetrics and Gynaecology,
Jessop Hospital for Women, University of
Sheffield*

MARTIN DUNITZ

To the women who have helped my research
and made this book possible

First published in the United Kingdom in 1984
by Martin Dunitz Limited, London

British Library Cataloguing in Publication Data
Coope, Jean
   The menopause – (Positive health guide)
   1. Menopause
   I. Title.   II. Series
   612'.655   RG186

ISBN 0 – 906348 – 60 – 9
ISBN 0 – 906348 – 61 – 7 Pbk

Phototypeset in Garamond by Input Typesetting Ltd, London

Printed in Singapore by Toppan Printing Company (S) Pte. Ltd.

CONTENTS

FOREWORD

by Prof Ian D. Cooke, Department of Obstetrics and Gynaecology, Jessop Hospital for Women, University of Sheffield

A general practitioner who engages in research to answer important clinical problems is an unusual person especially when the research is carried out over a number of years and the results are widely quoted in the literature. One must acknowledge this authority and such a person is Dr Jean Coope. This book has grown out of the knowledge generated by her interest in research and the human side of the problem presenting in her general practice.

Communicating results to a scientific audience is only one objective of research, another is to translate this research into terms that can be understood by women and their families who are all too frequently suffering from the impact of the menopause. An important element in management of the menopause is the explanation and counselling that is involved. Consultations are all too short and it is valuable to have available an easily understood manual for women and their partners to peruse at leisure.

This volume is an illuminating source of information for women at that time of life and presented with compassion and understanding. With its anecdotes and easy style I am sure it will be rewarding reading for any woman wondering about the background of the menopause.

INTRODUCTION

I hear so many opinions, worries and fears about the menopause, or 'change', from people coming to my surgery, or just in conversation:

'My wife's been awful lately. She can't say one decent thing – but I suppose you can expect her to be a bit off at a time like this.'

'These periods are a blessed nuisance. I wish the menopause would hurry up. It can't come soon enough for me.'

'D'you think hormones are a good idea? They do say that it's interfering with nature. What do you think?'

'You just have to wait till the children grow up – that's when you can enjoy yourself. Mind you, it was a bit of a shock when the eldest girl was expecting. But having grandchildren is very nice; you can hand them back afterwards. They come and play with us a lot but it's easier when you can send them back again.'

'I don't mind the flushes at all. They do say they do you good, worth a guinea each!'

'I have been a bit worried, not been feeling very well lately. You know, it's nice to talk to someone.'

'What about men? Is there such a thing as a male menopause?'

These are only some of the remarks men and women have made to me during the past few years. Although the menopause is not an illness, merely a life event, it seems to generate a lot of interest. Many women feel slightly apprehensive about it. They ask a lot of questions and I hope that reading this book may help to answer some of them.

When we are about fifty, women reach the menopause: our periods stop and we can no longer have children. Around 20 per cent of women leave the menopause behind them with only one reaction – a sigh of relief that the worry of contraception and the inconvenience of monthly bleeding are over. The rest experience hot flushes and sweats to a greater or lesser degree – and surveys carried out all over the world agree that these are the only characteristic symptoms of the menopause. This stage and the twenty years or so that follow are known by doctors as the climacteric, but in this book I talk about the menopause as that is the more well-known name. After the menopause your bones start a very gradual process of thinning down and you are more vulnerable to infection of the vagina. Ten per cent of women have severe symptoms, and many women suffer from loss of confidence, irritability and depression just before the menopause. Five per cent have sexual problems caused by the vaginal walls becoming dry.

The middle years can bring emotional and psychological problems too, as the balance of relationships within your family changes. Your parents are growing old and your children are struggling for independence. When they reach maturity and form partnerships of their own, you may suddenly find yourself catapulted into the generation of grandparents while you still feel like a teenager.

Middle age is a time for making all sorts of adjustments and adaptations. It is also a time for reviewing your attitude to your health and well-being. There is no doubt that the fuller your life is and the more active you are, the less you will be bothered by the menopause. If it does cause you problems, nowadays there is a wide range of treatments that can help. Drugs or hormone therapy can relieve your symptoms. At some stage an operation may be beneficial.

As a general practitioner and a regular counsellor at a Well Woman clinic I see hundreds of women with menopausal symptoms every year, and I deal with all these common physical and emotional difficulties. And in my role as a specialist on the menopause I have carried out research into the hormone and drug treatments now available. I find that most women want advice and reassurance on dealing with their symptoms as well as information about medical treatment they might need either during or after the menopause. My aim in writing this book has been to make that same information and advice my patients find helpful accessible to as many women as possible.

Ultimately the only person able to take charge of your health is *you*. Whatever the symptoms, the menopause is not a disease – your health is in your own hands. I shall try to show you how to keep it there.

Taking advantage of your opportunities

Depending on your point of view, the menopause and the twenty-five years that follow, can be regarded as either a problem or a privilege. What are you going to do with all those extra years? Looking after your family and particularly your partner may take up a lot of time and of course you are both getting older so there is more caring and it will take longer to do. Mothers and grandmothers are in short supply as more women go out to work. Children live in an increasingly violent and de-humanized environment and this may be reflected in their play and in behaviour problems, especially in the inner cities. This needs a human antidote and the loving and imaginative play a grandmother can give is especially valuable.

There are so many job opportunities for women, both paid and unpaid voluntary work. If you look around you will see many requests for help,

8

from schools (literacy programmes, mothering), old peoples' homes (shopping and visiting), the handicapped (reading to the blind), old folks' luncheon clubs, hospitals (library service, fund raising for equipment), patients' associations, local councils and political parties. The list is endless.

Adult education classes and craft training can be found in the local community. Art, music, drama, literature, business courses, gardening or working with beautiful furniture and antiques can enrich your life and give you a lot of pleasure.

You need to stay as healthy as possible so that you can enjoy these things. There are some illnesses that cannot be avoided but others are started or made worse by unhealthy habits like smoking, which you *can* do something about. You may need to economize and prune your lifestyle in certain directions in order to enlarge it in other areas. For instance, if you do not buy meat you may be able to afford asparagus. If you have to do without a car you could perhaps buy a swimsuit or a bike. Flexibility is the key to enjoyment.

Although you have reached a turning point, there is much that will stay the same – your relationship with the man in your life, your sex life, your friends, your job, and your part-time interests. Other things will improve – no more messy periods and no need to take precautions over lovemaking. Your role in life will change as your children grow to become equals and friends. But you are still necessary and can play a vital part in your family and community. You have a great deal to hope for and look forward to during these added years.

Keep well. Enjoy life!

1 WHAT HAPPENS AT THE MENOPAUSE

The menopause is a natural phase in the life of every woman and marks the end of the fertile years. Like the start of menstruation at puberty, it is triggered off by hormonal changes in the body. It should help you understand the changes that will happen to you during the menopause if I first explain briefly how menstruation works during the fertile years.

The stages of the monthly cycle

Not until about the age of thirteen do we start to have monthly periods – although of course some girls start at ten or eleven, others not until sixteen or even later. But from birth our bodies are preparing for the fertile years.

A baby girl is born with about two million egg-forming cells called follicles already in her ovaries – two pieces of pink-grey tissue about 1 in (2.5 cm) long situated either side of the pelvis. By the time she is eleven, a great many of these follicles will already have died – there may be only 300,000 or so left. When she reaches puberty, one or sometimes two follicles start to ripen every month under the influence of her hormones.

The pituitary gland, a small piece of soft tissue about as big as a cherry at the base of the brain, releases the hormone, or chemical messenger, which stimulates the follicles. This follicle stimulating hormone (FSH) causes the follicle to ripen and also to produce oestrogen, the female hormone. The rising level of oestrogen in the blood at first tries to stop the pituitary gland producing FSH. This is called negative feedback. But as the oestrogen levels go on rising the pituitary gland releases a wave of luteinizing hormone (LH) and some more FSH – positive feedback. Now ovulation is triggered.

At ovulation the ripened follicle bursts, the egg cell is released from the ovary and passes into the Fallopian tube, to travel to the womb where it is lost in discharge. The empty follicle develops into what is called a corpus luteum (yellow body) which makes oestrogen and another female hormone, progesterone.

Under the influence of oestrogen during the first half of the menstrual cycle before ovulation, the lining of the womb called the endometrium grows thicker. The combined effect of progesterone and oestrogen in the second half of the cycle after ovulation makes the endometrium thicken further and develop many tiny mucus glands as it prepares for a possible pregnancy. If pregnancy does not occur the corpus luteum dies, levels of

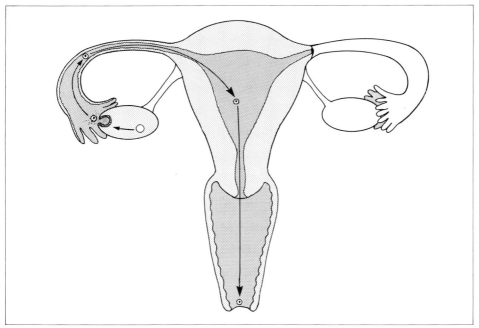

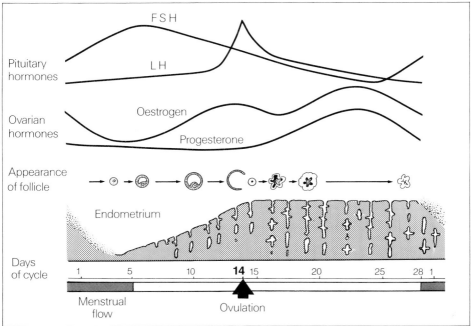

FSH

LH

Pituitary hormones

Ovarian hormones

Oestrogen

Progesterone

Appearance of follicle

Endometrium

Days of cycle

| 1 | 5 | 10 | **14** 15 | 20 | 25 | 28 1 |

Menstrual flow

Ovulation

The menstrual cycle

oestrogen and progesterone fall, and the endometrium is shed. With the shedding, blood that is stored in the endometrium rather like water in a sponge is displaced and then lost.

The shedding and blood loss are called menstruation, which is taken from the Latin *menses*, meaning month, and it occurs about every twenty-eight days in most women. However, there is a tremendous variation in the length of menstrual cycles. The shortest cycles recorded are eleven days, the longest 150 days. The length of each woman's cycle also changes between menarche (the start of the periods) and menopause. Young girls tend to have long cycles, of about thirty-five days, which shorten to an average of twenty-seven days by the age of forty-three and lengthen again to an average of fifty-two days by the age of fifty.

Changes in ovulation
By the age of forty-four a woman has about 8000 follicles left but only a few of these ripen to form egg cells. Although more follicle stimulating hormone is poured out of the pituitary gland than in younger women, ovulation does not happen at every cycle and without it no progesterone is made. Throughout the cycle the amount of oestrogen produced is also lower. But although the ovary produces hormones in smaller quantities it does not stop, even after the menopause.

Symptoms of the menopause – when do they start?
The menopause usually happens around the age of fifty but like the start of puberty this varies greatly in different women. You may stop having periods in your early forties or go on until you are fifty-three or four. It is rare for periods to continue after the age of fifty-five and many gynae-cologists would arrange an investigation for a woman having regular periods after fifty-four since having periods after this age may increase the risk of cancer of the womb (I discuss this more fully in Chapter 7).

When and why you start the menopause at any particular age is not fully understood, but the old idea that if you started periods early you will finish early too, and late starters continue longer than early starters is quite wrong. You may follow your mother's pattern, whatever that was. But it is not likely that you will miss the symptoms, whenever they begin.

Stages of the menopause
We talk about the menopause happening in three stages and associate particular symptoms with each one. Of course this is a broad way of looking at it and the stages of your menopause may vary a lot from this outline in length and timing of symptoms. The stages are known as:

- Pre-menopause
- Peri-menopause
- Post-menopause.

Pre-menopause From anything between three and ten years before your menopause you can begin to experience the following; the usual length of this stage is between three and four years:

1. Irregular and more frequent periods
2. Mood changes
3. Hot flushes in the week of the period.

Although people may tell you you should expect headaches and dizziness at this time, there is no medical evidence that they are symptoms of the menopause. You may have headaches at any age; my migraine actually got better during this period.

Peri-menopause This is the time when you stop having periods. The date of the last period is defined as the menopause. Because of the irregular periods and the timing being different for everyone, you can only be certain you have stopped having periods when you haven't had one for at least a year (see page 14). The symptoms of the post-menopause will of course happen around this time too.

Post-menopause Changes in hormone balance affect your body to a greater or lesser degree from now until old age; and in the post-menopausal stage you may have:

1. Hot flushes, or flashes
2. Sweating and palpitations
3. High blood pressure (not a visible symptom – but see page 21)
4. Weight gain and distension
5. Vaginal dryness
6. Osteoporosis, or thinning of the bones.

The first five symptoms happen immediately after the menopause, but the last occurs very gradually so that you probably won't notice any change until your seventies. Aching joints around the age of fifty, which people often put down to osteoporosis, are more likely to be the result of doing too much strenuous work.

The artificial menopause
If you have had a hysterectomy you will no longer have periods and some people call this the artificial menopause since the other symptoms do not happen at this time, but may later on when the normal menopause would be expected. I talk about this in more detail in Chapter 7.

Amenorrhoea This is the name for the stopping of menstruation at any time, from puberty to the menopause. If you stop having periods before the time you would expect the menopause you should see your doctor, who will check the cause for this: it can happen for various reasons including excessive loss of weight, as in the slimmer's disease, anorexia nervosa, because of thyroid disorder, or pituitary or ovarian disease. You will not have the symptoms of the menopause with amenorrhoea as your periods have been stopped by one of these other causes.

Although between 20 and 25 per cent of women pass through the menopause without any discomfort the majority experience some, if not all, of these characteristic symptoms to a greater or lesser degree. Some women are deeply affected, and nowadays there is much that can be done to help them, as I explain in this book. Others may be merely inconvenienced. But whatever your symptoms, the physical changes going on in your body can trigger emotional and psychological reactions and cause worry and depression, and these aspects of the menopause I shall deal with in more detail in the next chapters. Here I explain the main physical symptoms.

Irregular periods
This is the first and most obvious symptom of the menopause. In the years just before you reach the menopause, probably in your mid to late forties, you may find that your periods get more frequent and last longer. This is because the ovaries are no longer so efficient at producing oestrogen and progesterone. To counteract this, the pituitary gland produces higher levels of ovary stimulant (FSH, see page 10) and pushes the ovary into the next cycle ahead of time. It is very useful to mark off on a calendar when each period starts and how long it lasts, both for your own reference and as a useful record for your doctor.

As you approach the menopause you may have a brown discharge (see Chapter 5) or spotting of blood for a couple of days just before or after the period. Then the gaps between periods get longer, perhaps six weeks, three months, then six or eight months, until finally, when you are around fifty, your periods stop altogether. You may think that they have completely finished and then have another period a few months later. Some women have completely regular periods until they suddenly stop at the menopause. If you are under fifty you can say definitely that you are past the menopause if the last period was over two years ago. If you are over fifty you are past the menopause if your last period was over one year ago. It is now safe to stop using contraceptives.

There are some symptoms associated with irregular periods to watch out for, as you should tell your doctor if they happen to you.

Irregular bleeding   You may have a show of blood between your periods. This happens fairly often around the menopause, and it is easy to confuse the bleeding with irregular periods. But while irregular periods are completely normal, irregular bleeding is not. Any bleeding that occurs between

14

periods, after intercourse or after the menopause, is abnormal and you should tell your doctor about it. Irregular bleeding always needs investigating as it can be the first warning of operable cancer, and an early examination usually leads to a 100 per cent cure. So you should never put off having a check-up.

Margaret was the mother of two children. After she had turned forty-two, she noticed a slight spotting of blood between her periods. Sometimes it happened after sex. She came to see me and I examined her and carried out a cervical smear test. This was positive, that is, it showed a tendency of the cells to form cancer. She was referred to a gynaecologist and underwent a minor operation on the neck of the womb. Now, ten years later, she is absolutely fit, with no bleeding, and sex is normal. Her follow-up smear tests have not shown any recurrence.

Very heavy bleeding   This can be a great nuisance. If you have to go to bed during your periods and are unable to contain the bleeding with ordinary tampons and sanitary pads you should see your doctor. Sometimes the periods can be prolonged, with hardly any days when you are not bleeding. Again, see your doctor. The most likely explanations are:

Endometriosis: the red spots indicate the places where it may occur.

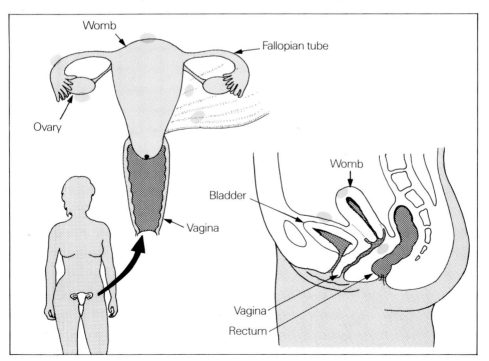

15

1. Over-stimulation of the womb lining by your natural hormones
2. Fibroids
3. An abnormal malignant growth.

Your doctor will check the haemoglobin level in your blood to make sure that you are not anaemic. He or she should then examine you vaginally to see if you have fibroids or anything else abnormal.

A fibroid is just a lump of muscle in the wall of the womb. It is not a cancer. But it can cause a lot of bleeding at the periods as it increases the area of tissue that bleeds. For this reason your doctor may recommend that the fibroids be removed, though they are in themselves harmless. Also we cannot be sure that a lump in the womb is a fibroid until it has been removed.

If there are no abnormal findings heavy bleeding can often be cured by a course of progestogen hormones, or by taking the drug danazol, which your doctor may prescribe for you for a few months. Danazol greatly reduces bleeding and it may stop the periods altogether. However, do not regard it as a contraceptive. You will still need to take the usual precautions.

Painful periods The medical term for this condition is dysmenorrhoea, and although it may happen at any age it is something to watch out for just before the menopause as this is the time when your health may be at a low ebb, so that you can be susceptible to problems with your periods. Again, do see your doctor if you have any worries on this score. Almost any disease of the womb and ovaries can bring on pain at the periods or just before they start, but the common causes are:

1. Infection
2. Fibroids
3. Endometriosis.

An infection will be cleared up by drug treatment, probably with antibiotics (see Chapter 5).

Fibroids As with heavy bleeding, fibroids are best removed if they are causing painful periods (see also Chapter 7).

Endometriosis This gets its name from the endometrium, the tissue that lines the womb (see page 10). Sometimes small pieces of endometrium grow in other parts of the pelvis, outside the womb, most commonly on the ovary, but also on the supporting ligaments of the tube or on the surface of the womb, bladder or bowel. This condition is known as endometriosis. It is common in premenopausal women.

16

Every month these pieces of tissue swell and bleed, but because the blood cannot escape, it causes pain rather like an abscess under pressure. The blood is partly absorbed but it may form dark brown cysts – chocolate cysts – on the ovaries; or the tissues become stuck together with scar tissue – adhesions – which can cause waves of pain in your abdomen and constipation or pain on moving the bowels.

The pain is often at its worst just before your period starts and on the first days of the period. Intercourse may be painful when the penis presses against the tender nodules behind the vagina. You may find a doctor's examination painful as the cervix is moved – but you will probably be given a laparoscopy (examining the abdomen with a tube like a telescope to confirm the diagnosis) under anaesthetic.

Endometriosis can cause a woman to be infertile. A number of self-help groups for women with this condition have been set up in the UK and addresses are given in the Useful Addresses section at the end of the book.

Treatment If your case is mild, you may be prescribed a course of progestogen, an artificially manufactured form of progesterone. For other cases danazol is an extremely effective treatment, as it prevents the pituitary gland stimulating the ovary and so stops ovulation. The nodules of endometriosis shrink and pain disappears. A high dose may be needed and this will stop both ovulation and menstruation. You may get side-effects such as a gain in weight, a rash or acne, but they will disappear once you have stopped the course of treatment – and most women are happy to put up with these temporary discomforts to be rid of the pain.

The alternative treatment is surgical removal of the abnormal tissue, or perhaps hysterectomy and removal of one or both ovaries if they contain cysts (see Chapter 7).

Hot flushes, sweats and palpitations

Although about 20 per cent of women do not experience hot flushes, they happen to most of us. Before the menopause they often happen only in the week of the period, while during the two years after the menopause they come on in earnest.

The flushes, or flashes, are harmless and they eventually disappear without treatment, but they can be a great nuisance. You suddenly feel hot all over and your face, neck and chest blush bright red. If you look in the mirror you may notice that you have turned red, but this does not always happen. A lot of women feel hotter than they look. The flush lasts for less than a minute and is sometimes followed by sweating and a feeling of coldness. You will find that you like to have the central heating turned down and that you do not enjoy hot weather.

Stress, tension, alcohol, tea and coffee and some drugs make flushes worse and they are commoner in hot weather. You can get help for these flushes if you find they are becoming intolerable.

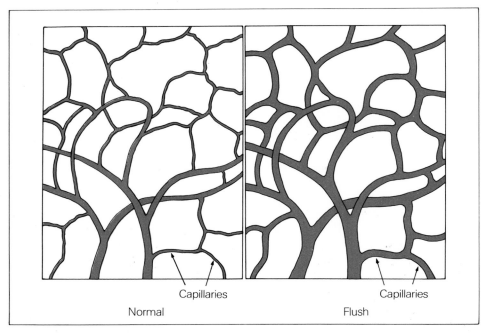

Capillaries   Capillaries

Normal   Flush

The blood vessel network contains about 60,000 miles (96,000 km) of capillaries. Normally *(left)* most are closed and empty of blood. During a flush *(right)* many open and fill up with blood, making the skin red.

Lilian came to see me very distressed because she could not cope with her job and her marriage was also affected by her problem. She was a teacher and had rather an unruly class of thirteen-year-old boys and girls. When things got difficult she flushed bright red and felt rather faint. This brought a few titters from the back of the class.

She had to wear cotton blouses or dresses all the time as even during the winter months she felt extremely hot. The central heating in the school did not help either. At night Lilian slept badly, usually waking up two or three times feeling very hot and drenched in sweat.

Her husband, also a teacher and rather a dominant man, was getting fed up as Lilian would throw the bedclothes all over him in the middle of the night and jump out of bed to have a shower and change her nightie. Their relationship had also been getting more difficult because Lilian was suffering from vaginal dryness and not enjoying sex as she used to. She often made some excuse to avoid it, saying that her period was on or she had a migraine.

Her husband at last insisted that she come to see me. I found she was a typical menopausal patient, with no other medical problem, and prescribed hormone treatment for her. This cured Lilian's hot flushes and also the vaginal dryness.

What causes hot flushes?

The exact cause of hot flushes is not known, but they are due to chemicals being released into the blood system at the time of the menopause. The blood vessels are sensitive to the chemicals and dilate, so blood rushes to the skin, making you hot and red. It is easy to imagine how overwhelming the effect of this can be when you think of the thousands of intricate blood vessels in your body.

The blood vessels are a network of hollow elastic tubes that branch and re-branch until the tiniest twigs are narrower than a hair. Blood is continuously pumped out from your heart through the arteries into the tiny vessels in the tissues and returned via the veins.

The reason anyone flushes is that suddenly something happens to close up the network. Perhaps you get frightened. The tiny vessels near your skin shut up altogether. You go pale because blood has been squeezed out of them. Consequently the pressure in the larger vessels rises, causing your blood pressure to go up. Your heart has to push harder to send the blood round. Then you relax. Blood flows back into your body's tissues, including the skin. You go red. You feel warm. Your blood pressure may fall. Your heart may beat faster because of nervous impulses trying to restore normal blood pressure.

The same effects can be caused by the release of the menopausal chemicals into the bloodstream, bringing about a hot flush. This explains why hot

The best clothing to wear when you expect flushes is light cotton, in several layers.

Take a tepid shower to cool you down when you are having flushes.

flushes can be accompanied by rapid changes in pulse rate. Your heart may suddenly begin to beat forcefully and fast, and you experience palpitations.

After a flush you may sweat in order to lose heat and reduce your skin temperature. You may feel faint or dizzy if you have a sudden drop in blood pressure, as your brain is momentarily deprived of sufficient oxygen to function properly.

Flushes can be unpleasant in a hot, humid climate, as evaporation of sweat from the skin is much less effective. During the hot British summer of 1976 we carried out a survey on twenty-five menopausal women who recorded the number of flushes they experienced each day. When the figures were examined together with the day's temperature, it became obvious that as the weather got hotter, the number of flushes went up. In cooler weather it went down.

Avoiding bad flushes
Hot flushes are harmless and most women do not consider they are worth treating. They usually come and go and disappear after a couple of years. There are however plenty of ways of cooling yourself down when you have a flush and so minimizing the effects. Here are some practical tips I have found useful for women who are getting a lot of flushes:

1. Wear several layers of light clothing so that you can easily adapt to the most comfortable temperature.
2. Don't wear a nylon bra – in fact in hot weather you may prefer to do without a bra at all.
3. Do without alcohol and coffee as far as possible since these tend to cause flushes.
4. If you are being given drugs for hypertension, find out from your doctor if they are likely to give you flushes; if so, you may be able to have the prescription changed.
5. If you can, have a tepid shower when you are feeling uncomfortably hot – it's more cooling and refreshing than taking a bath.

Only if you continue to have frequent flushes and sweats will medical treatment be necessary. Then hormone therapy will be prescribed (see Chapter 6). This counteracts the chemicals that cause blood vessel instability. Hot flushes and sweats stop. Before deciding on hormone therapy, you should have a medical check to measure your blood pressure and exclude conditions such as thyroid disease, which also causes flushes.

If you suffer from palpitations, small doses of beta-blockers, which are used for the treatment of high blood pressure and angina, can be prescribed.

Formication

Formication is an itchy sensation that you can get around the same time as the hot flushes. The name comes from *formica*, the Latin for ant, and the feeling certainly is rather like having itching ants all over your body. But it doesn't produce a rash like urticaria or eczema.

We are not sure what causes formication, although it seems likely that changes in blood circulation such as contribute to the hot flushes may be part of the reason, and anxiety could have an effect.

Treatment You will probably not need treatment as the formication will pass off on its own. If you can't stand the itchiness, though, see your doctor, who may prescribe either a course of tranquillizers or oestrogen; the latter is intended to alter the hormonal imbalance in the same way as the treatment for flushes does.

High blood pressure

Though your blood pressure may rise and fall quite suddenly at different times during the day, it does tend to get higher generally at the time of the menopause. But flushes are not caused by high blood pressure (also known as hypertension); and the condition can't be called a symptom of the menopause since you will not yourself be able to detect whether your pressure has increased – the only way to find out is to have it checked by your doctor, and it is important to do this now (I talk more about having medical checks in Chapter 4).

Between the ages of twenty and fifty women have, on average, lower pressure than men, although these differences are very small. Everybody's pressure rises as the arteries get narrower during middle age and between fifty and sixty the average pressures become equal in the sexes.

High blood pressure can lead to strokes, heart failure and kidney disease and it is associated with coronary heart disease. Although women are more tolerant than men of high blood pressure and have a lower death rate from coronary disease, they suffer equally from strokes.

Having your blood pressure checked

If the doctor checks your blood pressure and finds a reading greater than 160/100 he should arrange for several repeated readings. This can be done by the practice nurse and it often happens that the blood pressure drops so that the final reading is a lot lower than the first one. This probably happens because you are less anxious as you get used to having it checked. The average of four or five readings is obtained to give a true measurement. If you are under sixty and it is greater than 160/100 you are considered to have hypertension.

Your weight and height will be checked to see if you are overweight (a frequent cause of high blood pressure), and your urine examined to see if you have signs of diabetes or kidney disease. The doctor examines you for signs that the heart is affected and also to see if you have kidney disease which is raising the blood pressure. A blood test is often done at this stage to measure the level of salts in the blood, which may be affected by treatment. A chest X-ray or electrocardiogram may also be done to check the size and function of your heart.

It is important to tell the doctor about any medication you may be taking. Nasal drops or sprays, ephedrine tablets, drugs of the cortisone type, contraceptive pills and menopausal combined oestrogen-progestogen preparations, and anti-depressant drugs can all cause raised blood pressure. Although very high blood pressure needs treatment with drugs, mild hypertension can be helped by changing your diet and way of life:

1. Eat less sodium salt in food. Drink less alcohol, particularly beer. Eat less bacon and monosodium glutamate.
2. Take more potassium, which is contained in oranges, tomatoes and many vegetables and fruits.
3. Lose weight if you are more than half a stone heavier than the average (see the table in Chapter 4).
4. Avoid medications that raise blood pressure.
5. Take regular exercise. Although a temporary rise in blood pressure occurs when you exercise vigorously there is evidence that regular exercise improves the function of the heart and blood vessels.
6. Stop smoking. This has no direct effect on blood pressure but you reduce the risk of its most serious effects, stroke and heart attacks.

7. Find ways to relax. Stress often raises the blood pressure (see also Chapter 3).

Your doctor may decide that you need to take drugs to treat blood pressure but if you follow these guidelines a smaller dose is often effective. The commonest drugs used to lower blood pressure are thiazide diuretics which act by causing increased loss of salt and water in the urine, and beta-blockers, which block the effect of pressure-raising chemical messengers on the heart and blood vessels.

Putting on weight

Some women put on weight at the time of the menopause and just after it. There are two main reasons for this. First, as you get older your metabolic rate decreases and you burn up less energy. This coupled with a less active life and the same or a greater intake of calories than before, is bound to result in you putting on weight. At the menopause the amount of fatty tissue in your body increases and fat also retains fluid. Fluid retention makes for a noticeable and uncomfortable bulkiness.

The second common cause for putting on weight is connected with hormones. Hormone treatment can be prescribed for menopausal symptoms, as I have indicated (and I go into this in much greater detail in Chapter 6). A number of women receiving it hope that it will also improve their figures. It usually increases the size of the breasts temporarily and during the first few weeks of treatment some women complain of aching breasts, and they may need a larger bra. Unfortunately, you may gain weight overall on combined hormone treatments and particularly on pro-gestogens; some are closely related to the anabolic steroids which are body-building drugs. Oestrogen does not have the same effect. When I carried out a research study using an oestrogen-only preparation, we found that in most cases there was no weight gain, though there were other side-effects (see Chapter 6).

What should you do about gaining weight? If you can, pluck up the courage to slim with exercise and a calorie-controlled diet so that you can lose fluid as well as fat. Follow a sensible pattern, not a crash diet that has no long-term effect. I suggest ways of losing weight in Chapter 4.

If you are having hormone treatment and find you are gaining weight for this reason, your doctor may prescribe diuretic tablets. These are effective in getting rid of extra fluid and can safely be used together with hormone preparations.

If you find the weight gain more worrying than the menopausal symptoms, discuss this with your doctor, who will probably either change the preparation or, if it will be better for you, suggest you leave off hormone treatment for a while. Being very overweight is itself a potential cause of ill-health.

Distension

Menopausal women frequently complain of being bloated or blown-up, just as if they were about to have a period. Over the age of forty this bloated feeling gets more troublesome and varies with the time of day, being much worse in the evening.

What are the causes?

1. This condition is partly due to gas distending the bowels.
2. It is probably also caused by changes in your hormone balance. A similar condition occurs in the early weeks of pregnancy before the womb gets much larger, when there are big rises in progesterone. The hormone responsible at the menopause has not been identified.
3. Sometimes the distended stomach is due to fluid retention. Shifts in the distribution of body fluid occur during the day between the blood vessels and the other tissues. It is actually possible to gain a couple of pounds in weight each day due to fluid retention and lose it again at night.

Can distension be avoided? For gas distension I can only suggest you avoid foods you know give you wind such as large amounts of the pulses like dried beans and lentils. Otherwise, there is no effective way of preventing it.

You should not try to restrict your stomach by wearing a tight corset or force yourself into tight clothes – for example, skin-tight jeans. Change your clothes to looser styles such as a smock or kaftan later in the day if you begin to feel uncomfortable.

If you retain fluid and salt over a long time you can take diuretic tablets to get rid of the excess fluid.

Dryness and infection of the vagina and urethra

After the menopause, when the body's production of oestrogen has slowed right down, the lining of the vagina often becomes thin and dry. This is called vaginal atrophy. The vaginal secretions are scanty and less acid and infection is not easily resisted.

Vaginal atrophy can cause burning, itching, difficulty in having sex and sometimes yellow or brown discharge due to infection. Bleeding may occur, particularly if the lining is damaged by having sex after a long period of abstinence.

This problem is often worse in people who have had a hysterectomy, as all the secretions from the womb and cervix have been lost. If the ovaries have also been removed, the level of circulating oestrogen is further reduced and this alters the make-up of cells in the vagina so that it is more vulnerable to the entry of bacteria.

Similar changes can occur in the urethra and this will lead to burning and frequent passing of water.

Treatment These discomforts can easily be put right. Even a simple lubricant like K-Y jelly which you can buy over the counter may be quite effective, but the best treatment if the soreness continues is probably oestrogen cream or tablets. You will need a prescription from your doctor for these. Remember not to use oestrogen cream before sex, as it may be absorbed by your partner!

Early treatment can make a great deal of difference to your enjoyment of sex and to the success of your relationship.

Betty was a fifty-five-year-old patient who came to see me for a routine smear test. When I examined her it was really difficult to insert the speculum as the vaginal passage was so tight. When I talked to her about this, she admitted that she had not had sex for years. The membrane of the vagina was thin, shiny and red and started to bleed as I put my fingers in the opening. Betty had also been getting up frequently at night to pass urine, and the opening of the urethra looked red and sore. She was suffering from vaginal atrophy.

I prescribed oestrogen cream and a couple of months later, when she came to see me again, everything was quite different. She was having sex regularly, feeling well and I found that I could examine her easily with no pain or bleeding. On another visit, after more than a year, Betty told me she was still happy with the treatment.

Thinning of the bones, or osteoporosis

This is a process that begins during the years after the menopause, yet you will not notice it until old age. Your bones stay the same shape but become lighter and more brittle. The first sign of osteoporosis you will notice will be a very gradual loss of height. In old age there is a tendency for fractures to occur, usually in the wrists, legs or spine. If the spinal bones (vertebrae) become brittle they are squashed into a wedge shape and the spine becomes very curved. People who are laid up because they have an injury or a stroke lose bone density faster on the injured side.

The rate of bone loss is about 1 per cent per annum, but it is faster in women who have had their ovaries removed.

After the menopause you should not notice any major changes in your looks or figure for quite a long time. Although your ovaries are not very active, the adrenal glands, which are situated above the kidneys, now take over the production of hormones. They make a chemical called andros-tenedione, which travels in the bloodstream to the fatty tissues, where it is converted into oestrogen.

The continued supply of oestrogen is essential to avoid osteoporosis. It acts to prevent calcium, which is responsible for building and maintaining your bones, being lost from the bones and excreted in the urine.

25

What can you do to help?

You will lose bone faster if you are a heavy drinker, if you neglect your diet or take no exercise. But there is much you can do to slow down the process of osteoporosis:

1. Lead an active life to stimulate your adrenal glands into manufacturing more oestrogen. Exercise, excitement and sex are very good in this, as in other respects.
2. Make sure you have a sensible diet containing calcium-rich food (see Chapter 4).
3. You can take a course of hormone therapy. Even a couple of years' treatment will have a lasting good effect on your bones.

   An important study carried out in Denmark showed that women who received combined hormone treatment for three years and then stopped treatment lost bone more slowly than untreated patients. So even a short course of hormone replacement therapy may be worthwhile for you, though it is often more effective when taken from the time of the menopause for as long as possible (see Chapter 6).
4. Later, when hormones are not a suitable treatment, you may take body-building drugs. The anabolic steroids can be effective in treating osteoporosis.

After the menopause the adrenal glands take over from the ovaries to produce hormones.

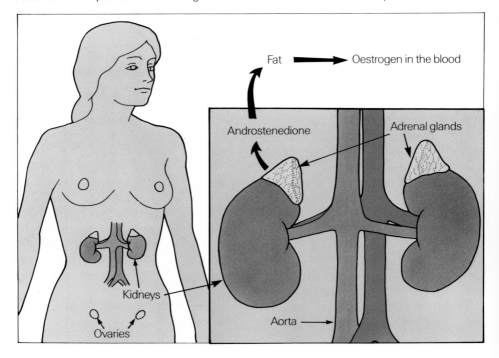

Regular exercise slows down thinning of the bones. Try a daily keep fit routine.

Will you have other symptoms at this time?

All the symptoms that I have described in this chapter are indications that you are going through the menopause. With the exception of irregular bleeding (not to be confused with irregular periods), they are the natural result of hormone changes and are easily treated if they become troublesome. Other problems that may occur around the time of the menopause but that are not directly related to it I describe in Chapter 5.

Many people blame the menopause for any number of completely unrelated complaints, and so I hope this book will help you identify your symptoms for what they are and decide how to deal with them.

However, if you are suffering from any symptoms at all that stop you doing what you want to do, it is worth paying your doctor a visit. You might have difficulty in sleeping, a pain in the chest or a change in the way your bowels are working. Although these problems probably have nothing to do with the menopause, they can happen around the same time. Women seem to be protected against many kinds of disease during the childbearing years and to lose some of their resistance at the menopause.

In the next two chapters I deal with the sexual, emotional and psychological difficulties that you may find are emphasized by the physical changes of the menopause.

2 THE MENOPAUSE AND YOUR SEX LIFE

A short time ago I gave a talk to a group of countrywomen at the Women's Institute in a tiny village on the fringe of the Pennine Hills in Cheshire. In the audience was a mixture of professional women, housewives and young mothers, aged anything between eighteen and eighty. After the meeting word went round among the locals that I had said something particularly shocking. What on earth was this daring statement that I had made? It was simply that women can go on having sex for as long as they want to – into their seventies and beyond! I had no idea that in the 1980s this would seem so revolutionary. Apparently there is still a widespread feeling that women ought to shut up shop sexually when they reach the menopause. There seem to be two schools of thought. 'It's all right for men – they can go on until they're ninety,' says one camp grudgingly, while the other breathes a sigh of relief: 'We deserve a rest from all that when we get to fifty.'

The plain truth is that sex can be enjoyable and exciting for women as well as for men – however old you are. It is a health-giving activity that gives an edge and a sparkle to life. Having said this, there are a few people who do have real problems during and after the menopause and in this chapter I shall try to suggest some ways of solving them.

Birth control over forty

An unwanted pregnancy is something that worries many women who are still fertile but have passed the normal age for childbearing. When you are over forty and have not yet reached the menopause there is still a reasonably high risk of becoming pregnant unless you use a reliable method of birth control. Remember that you will need to keep on using it until two years after the menopause if you are under fifty, or one year afterwards if you are over fifty, before you can be sure that you are infertile. Don't take chances – it's not worth it!

The Pill
The choice of contraceptive methods for the over-forties is the same as for younger women. Because of its convenience and simplicity the most popular contraceptive for women is certainly the Pill, and among younger women it is a safe and reliable method. It is, though, usually considered unwise for women over forty-five to take the combined Pill (containing

oestrogen and progestogen) because of an increased risk of blood clotting and heart disease. Many doctors refuse to prescribe the combined Pill to women over the age of thirty-five who smoke, as cigarette smoking greatly increases the risk of these diseases. But there are other oral contraceptives that most older women may use with safety.

The mini-Pill
The oral contraceptive most often recommended until the menopause is the mini-Pill or progestogen-only Pill. This has no effect on the liver and does not affect blood clotting. It has a failure rate of 3 per cent: out of one hundred women taking it for a year three will conceive. However, as fertility is not so high in women over forty this is not such a worry.

Always follow instructions on the use of contraceptives carefully. You should take the mini-Pill at the same time every day to ensure maximum effectiveness.

Side-effects   These are rare, but:
1. Sometimes women gain weight while taking the mini-Pill. This can be sorted out by your doctor, who may treat you with diuretic tablets or decide that you need a different method of contraception.
2. If you start to have irregular periods or bleeding between periods you should tell your doctor, and again a change to another method may be recommended.
3. Missed periods are very common on the mini-Pill and may worry you. To confirm whether or not you are pregnant you can take a pregnancy test on your urine yourself, or ask your doctor for one. If the test is negative your missed periods will be due either to the hormonal changes signalling the menopause or the effect of the Pill.

The 'morning-after' Pill
Only if you have had unprotected intercourse should you use the morning-after Pill. I do not recommend it as a regular contraceptive since it is not as reliable as the normal methods. You should take two tablets of a 50-microgram combined oestrogen-progestogen Pill as soon as possible after intercourse and repeat the dose in twelve hours. Ovran or Eugynon 50 are suitable preparations.

Bleeding should occur by the time the next period is due. If it does not, tell your doctor. The treatment is not recommended if you wait more than seventy-two hours after intercourse to take the first dose.

Is it wrong to use the 'morning-after' Pill?   There has been a lot of discussion in the press about whether prescribing the morning-after Pill is unethical, and anti-abortion campaigners have accused doctors of using it to procure an abortion illegally. Fertilization of the egg cell occurs in the outer end of the Fallopian tube a few hours after intercourse has taken place. The fertilized egg then travels along the tube to the uterus, taking four or five days to reach the uterine cavity. It lies free in the cavity for two or three days and is then implanted in the endometrium. The morning-after Pill works by changing the endometrium so that it is not receptive and the egg cell is not implanted. This effect is very similar to that of the IUD (see below) and the mini-Pill. So if these methods are acceptable there is no reason why the morning-after Pill should not also be accepted.

Another method which is sometimes used to protect against pregnancy after intercourse is for the doctor to insert an IUD into the uterus. This can be done up to five days after intercourse and is 99 per cent effective.

If you have had unprotected intercourse you need to see your doctor for either of these emergency measures.

Helen was fifty years old with an adopted daughter and had been married to a disabled man who had died five years previously. They had never managed to have complete sexual intercourse and she had adjusted to this, although she became rather depressed and overweight.

She recently came to see me looking quite different. She had changed her hairstyle, lost about 30 lb (14 kg) and looked beautiful but emotionally upset. She explained that she had met a marvellous man and fallen in love. They had been totally unprepared and had had unprotected intercourse the night before. She had had a period about a fortnight previously. I gave her the morning-after Pill and also fitted her with a diaphragm and wrote a prescription for spermicidal jelly. Ten days later her next period came and all was well.

Depo-provera

A six-weekly injection of Depo-provera (depot progestogen) is a very effective method of birth control. It is especially useful to women who are apt to forget to take the Pill regularly but are not suited to other contraceptives such as the IUD or the cap. This is not yet approved by the United States Food and Drug Administration but is widely used in other countries and is considered safe by the World Health Organization and International Planned Parenthood Federation. In the UK, Family Planning clinics use Depo-provera, but it is not yet approved for long-term use by the Committee of Safety of Medicines.

At the moment the discussions continue and whether it will be freely available everywhere is yet to be decided.

Side-effects Depo-provera can cause weight gain and irregular cycles, and it frequently leads to missed periods.

If your doctor decides you should not take any sort of oral contraceptive,

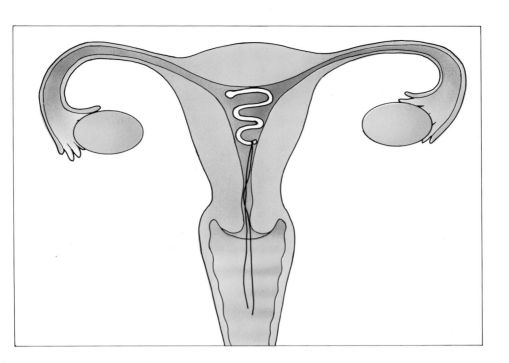

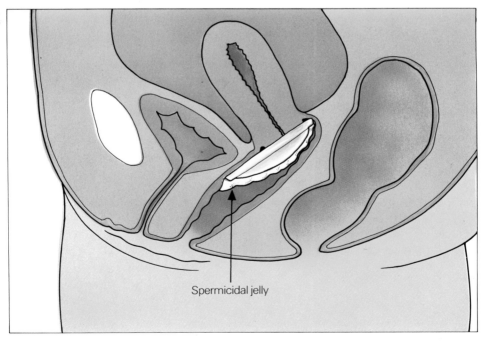

Spermicidal jelly

The IUD, *above*, and cap, *below*, are safe methods of contraception at the menopause.

you can use various other methods. Your doctor or clinic will give you advice about which will suit you best.

The intra-uterine device (IUD)

The IUD or coil is widely used by women over the age of forty and is trouble-free for the majority; though anyone with fibroids, irregular or heavy bleeding, or pelvic infection should not use this method. The coil works by preventing the fertilized egg being implanted in the womb. It has a failure rate of between 2 and 4 per cent so it is just about as effective as the mini-Pill. It is inserted by your own doctor or at a Family Planning or contraceptive clinic and it will need checking after two, six, twelve months and then yearly. It can be left in the womb until one or two years after the menopause, depending on your age (see page 14).

You should check that the tail of nylon thread can be felt before you have sex. If you can't feel it, use a sheath or cap and report to your doctor. The coil may have fallen out or retreated up into the womb, where it can be located by X-ray and then repositioned.

The cap or diaphragm

This is a rubber disc that is squeezed into place to block the vagina so that sperm cannot reach the cervix. It should be used with plenty of contraceptive jelly to seal the gap between the edge of the cap and the vaginal wall. You should put it into place before you make love, or before you go to bed, and remove it six hours or more after intercourse. It is a popular method of contraception with a failure rate of only 2 per cent if used correctly.

You will need to see your own doctor or a doctor at a contraceptive clinic, who will examine you to see which size cap you need. The doctor will show you how to insert it and check that you are using it correctly after a week's trial. Thereafter you should have a yearly check.

If you have a problem such as a prolapse (see page 69), the doctor may recommend a cervical cap, which is similar, but fits over the neck of the cervix.

The cap has the additional advantage of holding back the menstrual blood, so you may like to use it while making love when you have a period. This makes it especially useful at the menopause, when periods are unpredictable.

It also partly protects you against venereal infection and may reduce the risk of cervical cancer.

The sheath or condom

The sheath or condom is the most popular contraceptive method of all, as it is so easily available – it can be bought in packets from a pharmacy. It is like a second skin that is rolled over the erect penis before penetration and discarded after withdrawal. There are many types on sale and most are lubricated. You should use the sheath in conjunction with a contraceptive cream or pessaries, which are also bought at a pharmacy. The failure rate is about 3 per cent – though in people over forty it is only 1 per cent.

The main objection to the sheath or condom is that foreplay has to be interrupted when it is put on, and love-making may not be so spontaneous. Like the cap the sheath provides partial protection against infection.

Sterilization

You may feel that the only really sure way of avoiding a pregnancy is sterilization. This is obviously a major decision and should be discussed very seriously by you and your partner. If you consider sterilization, think of it as a permanent solution; do not go in for the operation with a lingering doubt about whether you want it, and the idea that you can in the last resort have it reversed. The operation can sometimes be reversed and conceptions have resulted in 50 to 75 per cent of cases after reversal operations in female sterilization (depending on the type of sterilization) and 33 per cent of cases after vasectomy or male sterilization. But reversal is a difficult surgical technique and success cannot be guaranteed, particularly after forty. Therefore, when you are thinking about sterilization, don't forget that you may later want a child with someone else. However far-fetched the idea is now, it is always possible that one of you may be widowed or your partnership will not continue into old age. Do not duck talking about these points when you discuss sterilization.

Once you have made your decision, you should talk it over with your doctor. If you are told sterilization would be suitable for you, make absolutely sure you and your partner know exactly what is involved, especially in the case of female sterilization, which can be a major operation.

Vasectomy

This is the sterilization of the man. Each male tube (vas) is cut and tied so that the sperm cannot travel from the testicles to the penis. This should not alter a man's sex life in any way – the only difference is that he does not produce sperm when he ejaculates. Nevertheless, some men find the idea of the operation psychologically disturbing. So it is a great mistake to try to talk your partner into having a vasectomy if he is against it. Once he feels pressure is being put on him and possibly that his virility is under attack your relationship, and especially your love life, is likely to be badly affected. If he agrees to the operation but is unhappy about it later, it will be wise to seek counselling either from your doctor or one of the organizations listed at the end of this book.

Vasectomy is a minor operation which can be performed under local anaesthetic. The man can leave the hospital immediately and needs no period of convalescence. It is also a cheaper operation than female sterilization. Samples of seminal fluid are taken about three months later, after twelve to thirty ejaculations, depending on the hospital. Tests are made to check for the presence of sperm, and after two negative tests it will be permanently safe to have sex without any other contraceptive.

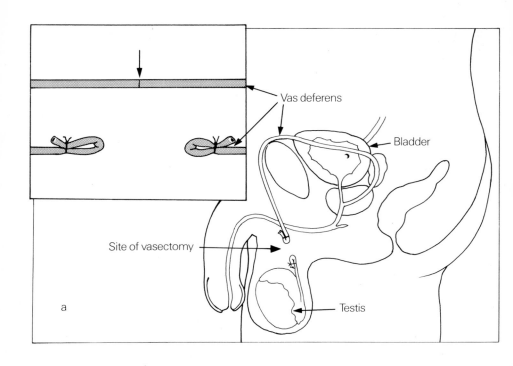

Vas deferens

Bladder

Site of vasectomy

Testis

a

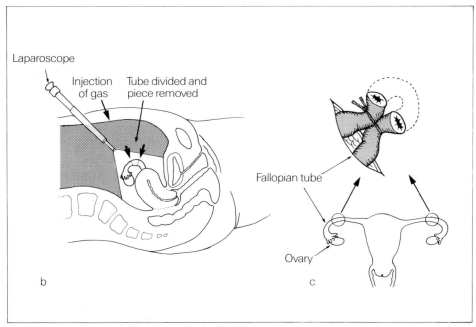

Laparoscope

Injection of gas

Tube divided and piece removed

Fallopian tube

Ovary

b

c

Methods of sterilization: *a*, vasectomy, *b*, laparascopic sterilization, *c*, tubal ligation.

Female sterilization

There are four methods of sterilizing a woman, and all remove the risk of pregnancy immediately. Before you agree to the operation, you should make very sure which one has been recommended and what the chances of reversal are. The four methods are:

1. Laparascopic sterilization, which usually involves having the tubes cauterized, or sealed
2. Having the tubes tied, called tubal ligation
3. Having the tubes removed, called salpingectomy
4. Having the womb removed.

Which means of sealing the tubes is used will depend on the facilities available at the hospital you attend. Your tubes should only be removed if your doctor decides they are in danger of becoming or are diseased.

The legal position for married women in Great Britain is that if you are living together the consent of both you and your husband is required for sterilization; though if sterilization is necessary on medical grounds, the spouse's permission is not needed. In Canada and most states in the USA the spouse's permission is not required; in some sterilization is funded by the federal department of Health and Human services, and in this case a detailed consent form must be signed by the applicant.

Laparascopic sterilization   In this operation the tubes are cauterized, that is, sealed so that the egg will not pass into the womb. It is carried out under a general anaesthetic, or a local anaesthetic with a sedative.

Two cuts about ½ in (1¼ cm) long are made in the abdomen. Gas is injected into the abdominal cavity through a needle so that the gynaecologist can see the tubes clearly. A laparoscope, which is a bit like a slender telescope with a light, is introduced through the centre cut, and a small pair of forceps through the other. When the forceps grasp the Fallopian tube an electric current is passed through them and the tube is cauterized. Each tube is cauterized in two places, and sometimes the intervening portion of tube is removed.

Reversal of this operation is not often successful, although a recent modification avoiding cauterization increases the chances. Instead of the current sealing the tubes, they are blocked by rubber grips or clamps.

After the operation   You return home within twenty-four to forty-eight hours and you will not feel any great discomfort. The worst that you might experience is some soreness around the cuts and a slight depression, such as is common after any minor operation. Both these effects are shortlived. You will be able to have sex within a week of coming home.

Tubal ligation   No heat is used to tie the tubes in this operation. It is carried out under general anaesthetic and you will be in hospital for up to five days. A cut 2–3 in (5–8 cm) long is made at the top of the pubic hairline and the middle portion of each Fallopian tube is tied and cut out.

The advantage of this operation over laparascopic sterilization is that it is easier to reverse as the two ends of the tube can be brought together again in microsurgery.

After the operation   When you go home you will need to take life easily for about a month. Make sure you don't lift heavy things or go in for violent exercise, sport or gardening. Let your partner, family and friends do the heavy work until the scar is properly knitted.

Salpingectomy is the technique whereby both tubes are removed. Again it is carried out under general anaesthetic and your stay in hospital will be about five days. Each tube is tied at the uterus end, and the rest of the tube is removed. This operation is not reversible.

You should go carefully after the operation for a few weeks, as I suggest above, for tubal ligation.

Hysterectomy is the removal of the womb. The medical profession terms this a method of female sterilization, but of course the operation is not done primarily as a contraceptive measure but if your womb is in some way diseased. I describe hysterectomy in Chapter 7.

Pregnancy

Since periods become irregular just before the menopause, it is often difficult to know how to interpret a missed one. Up to now you have probably relied on this sign to tell you whether or not you are pregnant.

Testing for pregnancy
If you miss a period and think you may be pregnant, it is important to check. You can buy pregnancy testing kits at a pharmacy or your doctor can arrange a test for you. In our practice we carry out dozens of pregnancy tests each year for women who are not sure whether they are pregnant or menopausal. Whether you do the test at home or go to the doctor, you will need to wait six weeks after your last period and then take a sample of early-morning urine.

There are disadvantages to relying on this easy method though:

1. The test is only 98 per cent accurate and sometimes women who are pregnant have a negative test.
2. A false positive result occurs in some women at the menopause. This is due to the high level of hormones released from the pituitary gland, called gonadotrophins, which are present in the urine.

Therefore, even if your test is negative, if you are at all unsure about whether you are pregnant it is wise to see your doctor for a clinical examination.

Do you want a baby?
During this period you must think over your own attitude to a late pregnancy. Would you be happy to have a baby at this time of life? What does your partner feel about it? What are things like at home? Are you the sole breadwinner?

Although in Western countries the risk to the mother is very low – in the UK only one in 10,000 women die in childbirth each year – it does double over the age of thirty-five. This is because women in this age group are more liable to problems such as:

1. High blood pressure and the maturity-onset type of diabetes.
2. Complicated delivery caused by twin pregnancy, which is more frequent in older mothers.
3. An abnormal position of the baby.
4. The risk of having an abnormal child rises with the age of the mother and if you are over forty there is a greater than 2 per cent risk of having an abnormal child.
5. There is an increased risk of mongolism, and if you have a family history of this disease the chances of your child having it are higher.

What action should you take?
There are, of course, only two options, either to have the baby or seek a termination of pregnancy. The immediate shock of finding that you are pregnant can be so great that it unbalances your ability to make decisions. If the doctor confirms that you are pregnant it would be a good idea to talk over the alternatives with him or her and then go home and discuss them with your partner. Later the doctor may see you both together and you can make a decision.

Termination of pregnancy is legally available for two-thirds of the world's population. Just over 2 per cent of American women and 1 per cent of British women aged fifteen to forty-four have legal abortions each year. The legal requirement for an abortion in Great Britain and Australia is the opinion of two doctors that continuation of the pregnancy would be a risk to the mother's life or health, or the health of existing children in the family, greater than if the pregnancy were terminated, or there is a substantial risk that the child might be born severely handicapped. In Canada a committee of three hospital doctors makes the decision and policy varies from hospital to hospital. In the USA abortion is legal and most states permit it at the woman's request; but termination is not allowed after six months unless it is necessary to save the mother's life or health.

If you feel that an abortion is the right course you should discuss it with

Having a baby later in life can give great pleasure.

your doctor who can then refer you to a specialist or a clinic. If you are married they would wish to obtain your husband's consent, although this is not legally necessary in the UK.

Termination of pregnancy

Abortion is much safer during the early weeks of pregnancy and it is important if you decide on it to arrange the operation with your doctor as soon as possible. If your pregnancy is discovered later than twelve weeks on, a termination will be a lot more difficult and this may affect your decision.

Occasionally sterilization is offered after termination of pregnancy. This may seem useful as you have only one period of admission to hospital. In practice it is not such a good idea as you may feel rather unsettled and unwell after an abortion.

You will be in hospital not more than forty-eight hours for this operation but you are likely to feel the after-effects for some time when you go home. The hormonal changes caused by the pregnancy can leave you feeling under the weather, and of course you may well be depressed. Your partner should give you plenty of sympathy and support until you have pulled through, but do talk to your doctor if you feel you need more help.

If you have weighed up all the pros and cons and decide to go ahead with having the baby you can have a test at sixteen weeks to make sure it is normal. This is an amniocentesis. A sample of the fluid surrounding the baby is withdrawn, a culture of the baby's cells is allowed to grow in the laboratory, then examined for abnormality. If the baby is not normal, a termination may be arranged.

I know several women over forty who have chosen to go on with their late pregnancies and have adjusted well to healthy babies. And a bonus for women who give birth over forty is that they tend to be protected from the symptoms of the menopause!

Olive was forty-five years old and had a teenage son and daughter. She came to see me because of irregular bleeding and was referred to a gynaecologist, who found nothing abnormal.

A few months later she complained of swelling and when I examined her I found that she had an abdominal tumour reaching to just below the navel. When I listened to the 'tumour' through a stethoscope, I could hear it ticking regularly!

Olive went to the hospital and a scan showed that she was eighteen weeks pregnant. Termination would have been risky and she decided to go on with the pregnancy, although she felt very anxious about whether the baby would be normal. She was safely delivered of a healthy boy and the family are delighted with their young brother.

Enjoying sex after the menopause

So far I have talked about the issues that will occur just before and during the menopause. As I said at the beginning of this chapter, there is no reason why you shouldn't enjoy a satisfying love life as long as you want after the menopause. But you may find some difficulties that can affect both your own and your partner's enjoyment. These need to be approached tactfully. If for any reason you are having sex less frequently and either or both of you are unhappy about it, your relationship can be greatly strained. So make sure you discuss any resentments openly and if they can't be resolved between you, don't be afraid to ask for counselling from your doctor or one of the marital agencies listed at the end of this book. Further excellent advice on this subject can be found in *Enjoy Sex in the Middle Years* by Dr Christine Sandford, also in this series.

Overcoming physical disabilities
I have already described the physical difficulties associated with the menopause in Chapter 1. Here I suggest remedies for any that may affect a woman's sex life after it.

Dryness of the vagina   After the menopause the vagina shrinks and its lining gets thinner and more fragile so that penetration by the man's penis may be painful and cause bleeding. Use lubricants such as K-Y jelly, or spermicidal jelly; if these do not help you should see your doctor, who will prescribe hormone cream or tablets to help your sex life return to normal.

Illness   Disabilities not directly connected with the menopause may be an obstacle to your enjoyment. You or your partner may have an illness affecting your sex life. If, for example, you are suffering from diabetes or being treated for high blood pressure, you can experience loss of libido.

It is not unknown for sexual problems in a partnership to be put down to the woman's menopause when they are really due to the man's ill health. If your partner has had a major illness, or perhaps a heart attack, the doctor may have forgotten to tell him when it is safe to have sex and he may be too anxious to experiment. Do try to talk to your partner sympathetically and ask him to get some definite medical advice on this point.

Diabetes can cause impotence in some men. Sometimes operations such as removal of the prostate can also lead to sexual problems. A prostate operation does not, however, mean that your partner will become impotent, and he should ensure beforehand that this will not happen unless absolutely necessary. Again, you should ask your doctor to speak to you both about what to expect and how to deal with any problems that may arise. It is always worthwhile trying to keep your sex life active. Remember, it is not necessary for men to have an emission every time. Bearing this in mind, it may be easier for your partner to have an erection next time. Hand stimulation may be necessary in older men.

Disability   If one of you is disabled or has a bad back, you may need to change the way you make love or try out new positions. Try to be adaptable, for if you can enjoy sex it will make a great difference to your life. Apart from being fun, it can greatly reduce tension and hold your relationship together. There are some useful pamphlets on how to manage when one of you is physically disabled, and these can be obtained from organizations such as SPOD in the UK or counselling agencies in other countries (Sexual and Personal Relationships of the Disabled: see Useful Addresses, page 99).

Being alone   If for some reason you can't have sex with your partner, or if you are alone, it is possible to get a lot of satisfaction and relief from masturbation. Please don't believe the old wives' tales about masturbation causing illness or mental imbalance, or being an indication of the fact that you can't enjoy sex with a partner. The opposite is true. If you can have an orgasm when you masturbate, you are a normal, sexually healthy person.

Sex and the male menopause

Does the male menopause exist? Obviously, as men do not have periods, in a literal sense, the idea of a male menopause is nonsense. Men who are healthy and sexually active can go on producing sperm and father children into their eighties. However, most men have more erections and find it easier to reach a climax in their teens and twenties than in their sixties, and studies have shown a gradual decline in male sexual function over the age of fifty or sixty. In this sense, men's sex lives may become 'menopausal' during the middle years, but the effect is not directly related to age. Often lifestyle has its influence, for example, greater pressures and preoccupations at work, or an increase in weight, or alcohol consumption can interfere with regular sex. A lack of confidence or a degree of aggressiveness are not unusual if a man feels he is losing his youthful figure and attractiveness. If you notice some of these signs in your partner you should realize he needs consideration too. Sympathetic discussion and determination to keep your relationship a happy, loving one are the basis for the right sort of approach.

There is a tiny group of middle-aged men who have high FSH levels like menopausal women (see Chapter 1) and whose testes do not function normally. They are unable to get an erection or produce adequate sperm, feel fatigued and may get hot flushes. They are cured by a course of testosterone (male hormone) or pituitary hormone, and after a time they may be able to produce adequate levels of testosterone themselves again. Their condition is reversible, and therefore different from the female menopause.

Loss of libido

The problems of illness and ageing I have mentioned before culminate in one fundamental effect on your love life – loss of libido. Desire is the first essential for successful sex and loss of libido is one of the great problems for both men and women as they get older. Sometimes drugs for treating high blood pressure or other conditions can lower the libido. Or it can be a symptom of depression. If you suspect either of these causes you should ask your doctor. It may also be necessary to check that you have not developed diabetes or thyroid disease, either of which can bring on this problem.

Besides physical difficulties at the time of the menopause, you may have worries that result in loss of interest in sex. Arousal starts in the mind – and it's difficult to be interested in sex if you're anxious or depressed. You may have problems with money or your family occupying your mind.

Another hazard of the middle years is boredom creeping in so that love-making becomes more and more infrequent.

How to overcome loss of libido Many people have their own methods of preventing boredom – such as fantasy, or dressing to attract each other or going away for a weekend. If you have allowed your sex life to get less

regular, and are unhappy about that, do consider these ways of brightening it and giving yourself and your partner more pleasure. 'Use it or lose it' is a remark that can be applied to your sex life. If you and your partner get out of the habit of sex it may be difficult to start again. Boredom is quite curable, and has nothing to do with the menopause. All you need is a little imagination.

If you have no other medical problem, yet the ways I suggest above don't work for you, you might consider trying hormones, which can be given for loss of libido. A mixture containing oestrogen and male hormones can be helpful.

The most effective preparation is a mixture of testosterone and oestrogen which is made up in a small pellet and implanted under the skin (see Chapter 6). The effect lasts for three or six months depending on the dose given, and afterwards you may need to have a repeat dose. A mixture of male and female hormones is also contained in the preparation Mixogen, which is taken by mouth.

Male hormones usually increase libido, but they occasionally cause side-effects such as growth of hair on the face and deepening of the voice, and this is prevented by giving extra oestrogen at the same time.

Self-image
As you go through the menopausal years you may find that your life seems to have turned topsy-turvy. You feel as your children grow up and realize their own sexual potential that you have changed overnight from being young to being a mother-in-law or a grandmother. You become one of the older generation with a third generation below you, and this may be rather unnerving and result in a loss of confidence about yourself as a woman. Just because your periods have stopped there is no need for you to alter your role. In fact the menopause can be a great boon. You are free of the messiness and inconvenience of bleeding; you no longer need bother about contraception; you have not lost your sexuality or your looks, and with good health and vitality and an active sex life you should be able to stay young for a long time to come.

In Chapter 4 I suggest ways you will be able to prolong an active life, sexual and otherwise. But first I shall explain some of the emotional and psychological effects of the menopause.

A relaxing break with your partner can restore enjoyment of sex for both of you.

3 RELATIONSHIPS AND ANXIETIES

Middle-aged men and women tend to carry the heaviest burdens in the community, as they are at the peak of their earning capacity and often responsible for supporting both the young and the old. The menopause can bring extra problems just when you are using all your resources to the full.

Most people will recognize it as a turning point. But what some fail to realize is that it is a sensitive time not just in their own lives but for all the family as well – a time when everyone needs to exercise a lot of understanding.

In this chapter I want to talk about both the personal psychological effects the menopause may have on you, and the way your relationships are likely to be influenced.

Your children

At this time your role in life is changing fast: as you are becoming menopausal, your children may be entering adolescence. They, like you, will have swift and unpredictable changes of mood triggered off by alterations in hormone balance. When emotions are volatile it can be difficult to cope with the new situations that will undoubtedly arise as your children move into the fertile years and you leave them behind. Anxiety on both sides can result in aggression, and this can lead to upsetting quarrels.

What pressures will you experience? Your children are approaching adulthood and getting ready to leave home. Your feelings about them have got deeper and richer as you have watched the emergence of their independent personalities, and sometimes your caring leads to resentment on their part. Their behaviour can often seem rebellious or indifferent to you after all the years of love and hard work you have given them. You may suddenly feel devalued.

Sooner or later, your son or daughter will bring home a girlfriend or boyfriend. The first visit can be quite tense as the two generations size each other up. Try to take it calmly and look at your visitor through the eyes of your child, remembering that he or she is being weighed up by an equally critical family on the other side. This is probably something more than just a light-hearted relationship, otherwise the introduction would not have been made, so try not to judge too rashly. You may not think the stranger is the perfect son or daughter-in-law, but the chances are that your children know who will suit them better than you do, and the sooner you accept this fact, the happier your family will be.

How can you help the family unity?

1. Although you will obviously want to avoid major family rows where possible, it is important that you let your feelings come out somehow. Don't store up your petty grievances so that they get out of proportion and finish by triggering an enormous outburst. Try to discuss family issues calmly and reasonably and get everyone to agree on acceptable solutions.
2. Let the family know your own physical and emotional problems. It is pointless to try and keep the menopause a secret from teenagers. They will be much more understanding about your occasional uneven temper if you take them into your confidence. But don't trade on it and become a nagging, bad-tempered mum!
3. If you find that you can't always behave as you'd like to towards your children and that things are getting on top of you, you may benefit greatly if you set aside some time every day when you can be alone. Privacy is very important, and mothers are often denied it. You might use the time for relaxation therapy, assertion training, yoga, meditation – any of which you can learn at local adult institutes – or a long walk or drive by yourself.
4. Develop new interests and friendships to carry you through these difficult years. A sense of self-esteem is very important for your health, and a great gift to impart to your children.

Your grandchildren
The next great event on the horizon may be the birth of your first grandchild. The pattern of your life is becoming more complicated. Although you may be delighted with the new arrival, being a grandmother can alter the way you think of yourself quite drastically. Overnight you have moved into the next generation – but this is not the same thing as growing old. You will be surprised with what ease you adapt to your daughter's or son's baby and the tremendous sensual joy you can experience from playing with a young child. The birth of a grandchild can be particularly welcome as you know you can no longer have another baby yourself.

The childless woman
If you do not have children by the time you have reached the menopause, the sight of a young mother and baby can be a sad reminder of the fact that you have never conceived. The fantasy child who has perhaps occupied a place in your mind for so many years has to be given up.

Taking up yoga will teach you to relax and iron out anxieties.

You should not repress your maternal feelings – unused love and energy can turn into self-pity and bitterness. You have plenty to give. Consider running a nursery or play school, or taking up other kinds of valuable community service such as paying visits to hospitals or old people.

Your parents

You may already be looking after your own or your partner's parents. They may depend on you for company as well as for practical help. It is important that they should not feel humiliated by this reversal of role – after all, you were once dependent on them – and you will probably have to exercise a great deal of tact and understanding in your dealings with them.

You will have prepared yourself for the loss of your parents. When they die, you may feel your own death has come a great deal nearer. Do not suppress your unhappiness at this time. It is far better to allow full expression of your emotions than to bottle them up.

In trying to cope with your feelings of grief and the loss of people who have done so much to shape your life, you may even find yourself talking aloud to them. This can be worrying, and people have often asked me if talking to the dead is a sign of mental breakdown. I reassure them that it

46

is not – in fact it can help to prevent depression as it releases the emotional tension that builds up.

The man in your life

Though there is no such thing as a male menopause (see Chapter 2), men too have to cope with a changing self-image as they approach middle age. Like women, they start to compare their bodies with the slimness and vitality of youth and they can be depressed knowing that they will not live for ever and seeing the gap between what they would like to achieve and what is possible. They may respond by asserting their virility and vitality in different ways, perhaps by taking up jogging and the cult of physical fitness, possibly by having an affair with a younger woman. Although some partnerships break up at this time, many survive – even the ones that might not have been everything both parties hoped for.

You may have longed for a more exciting partner – the ideal man in your imagination. You may even have been prepared to risk everything to find this man of your dreams. But with the approach of the menopause, perhaps you start to think that the chances of Mr Right coming along are more and more remote and say goodbye to your fantasy.

A lasting, caring relationship will provide happiness and support for years.

The menopause is a time for coming to terms with what you have already achieved. If you can look at your relationship objectively, you should understand its true worth and find that you can enjoy a great deal of happiness together. The relationships you have formed by the time you reach the menopause are usually the starting point for your future life. As you get older, you will probably find that your bond with your partner gets stronger. You can look forward to retirement together enriched by hundreds of shared memories and experiences. You will be thrown into each other's company far more than ever before in your lives, so you will need to work together to provide each other with plenty of love and support.

When things go wrong   If your partnership does seem to be foundering – and this is not uncommon around the time of the menopause, with the pressures and anxieties I have outlined in this chapter taking hold – it may be a relief to discuss your worries with a counsellor, or your doctor.

Janet was a big, motherly woman of forty-eight who came to see me quite often with all kinds of problems. At the first visit she complained of vaginal discharge. She was investigated and then treated with a course of pessaries. About two weeks later she came in and asked for sleeping tablets. The next three visits were concerned with her daughters – one had trouble with her weight and the other had bad period pains. After that Janet complained of severe headaches, dizziness, tiredness and palpitations, particularly during the night. She asked me if she needed hormone treatment.

Finally we got to the root of the problem when Janet admitted that she thought her husband was seeing another woman. She had asked him about it and he told her that her suspicions were the first sign of mental illness. Naturally this made her even more anxious and she needed a great deal of reassurance that she was not going mad.

I asked her husband if he could possibly come to the surgery and talk over Janet's problems. After a good deal of persuading he agreed, and we had a long chat during which he denied any kind of infidelity and seemed quite surprised at his wife's reactions and symptoms.

Several weeks later, he was spotted in a hotel with another woman and in the end he admitted the truth. When Janet came to see me about this she started to cry and was obviously very distressed, but some of her most frightening symptoms, such as the palpitations, had disappeared. She said that it was a relief to know the truth.

Eventually the marriage split up and now at last she has found another partner. Janet is very busy making a new life with the man she loves and caring for his two children in addition to her own daughters, who have quickly settled down with their stepfather.

No relationship can be looked upon as absolutely permanent and you have to face the possibility of your partner dying before you. If you are suddenly left alone at the time of the menopause you will feel as if half your being has been sliced away and you will probably experience an undermining of your confidence. This is the time when you must turn to people around you for comfort and support.

Whether you have been widowed or your partnership has split up, you may well find a new partner during these years, and the adjustment to a different relationship and probably a new family will take some effort on both your parts.

A new partner
The balance of relationships within the family often shifts around in a surprising way during the middle years. A second marriage or partnership will bring a whole new set of relationships with it – you could become a stepmother to your new partner's children, and he could be a stepfather to yours.

At this stage it is important to give support to your own children, if they are with you, while they live through the experience of the loss of their father. Even if he has been a bad husband and father, it is hurtful to belittle him in front of them – this will give them a low self-image as they are still part of him and will identify with him to a certain extent. They will feel that you are rejecting them too and they may turn against you in order to protect themselves from criticism. Your role as a mother is still crucial in middle age, although the pattern and balance of the family has shifted, rather like a mobile that is moving in the breeze.

Worrying about your role

Worries about these altering relationships and doubts about yourself as a woman while you are going through the menopause can cause anxiety and depression around this time. They are not symptoms of the menopause themselves, and so are not inevitable, as many people think. The two states are distinguishable from each other and you may experience one without the other.

Anxiety
This is a state with definite symptoms. Some are the same as signals of the menopause and for that reason people may wrongly assume they are suffering from menopausal symptoms when they are acutely anxious. If you have all the following symptoms, or most of them, at a time when your worries such as I have outlined in this chapter are getting on top of you, then you may be suffering from anxiety.

The symptoms

1. Palpitations or high pulse rate
2. Sweaty palms
3. Hot flushes, or flashes, or feeling cold
4. Diarrhoea
5. Frequency in passing water
6. Dry mouth and difficulty in swallowing
7. Difficulty in sleeping
8. Muscular weakness or trembling.

Most of these symptoms caused by anxiety are due to increased adrenaline (epinephrine) being pumped from your suprarenal glands.

How can you overcome anxiety? First, you should try to overcome your anxiety by self-help methods – learn to relax and control your breathing when you are feeling anxious or upset (*Anxiety and Depression* by Prof Robert Priest, also in this series, will help you learn the relaxation techniques); seek the support of your partner and friends over things that are worrying you; let your insomnia take care of itself (see page 61). The symptoms of anxiety pass away when you have learnt to deal with the causes.

If you cannot relieve the anxiety by yourself, go to your doctor. Tranquillizers or beta-blockers, which slow the heart rate and reduce nervous tension, may be prescribed for you; and you will find discussing your state with someone trained to recognize and deal with the symptoms is itself a help.

Depression

This is a very common condition in all types of people – one large study found that 25 per cent of the British population was suffering from it, only half of whom had been diagnosed by their doctors as having an emotional illness; women are twice as likely to be suffering from depression as men, and for the reasons I have already discussed it is particularly common around the time of the pre-menopause, just before the periods finish. All the same, you should not *expect* to suffer from depression. Feeling a little low from time to time is normal in anyone and I hope from what I say here you will be able to distinguish which your state is likely to be.

Diagnosing depression Depression can be difficult for a doctor to diagnose, as people suffering from it may produce other symptoms. These are unconsciously induced or psychosomatic illnesses. For example, what appears to be a straightforward case of gall-bladder disease with abdominal pain and nausea may actually be a case of depression. The recognizable symptoms of depression are:

1. Feeling low, burnt-out or flat
2. Difficulty in sleeping, particularly in the early morning
3. Continual tiredness
4. Difficulty in making decisions, even minor ones such as what to buy when out shopping
5. Loss of interest in sex
6. Guilt feelings
7. Feeling sad and perhaps wanting to cry often
8. Sometimes a depressed person may eat, drink, or smoke a lot, and these excesses will cause other symptoms, such as nausea or dizziness, which mask the original problem.
9. Alternatively you may lose your appetite altogether and begin to lose weight.

Coping with depression   What you need most when you feel depressed is something to bolster your ego, such as a happy relationship or a satisfying career. Don't hold back from seeking comfort and affection from your partner. The fact that you ask for help at this time can have a very positive, strengthening effect on your relationship.

Fill your new-found free time with a pastime that attracts you.

If you feel the need for more stimulus to jolt you out of your state, take steps to find a new occupation – a job in a field that particularly interests you (see opposite), perhaps voluntary work, or a hobby you might start at an adult education class, such as taking up a language or doing pottery or painting.

Less fundamental boosters – a good holiday or weekend away, some new clothes – can give you a tremendous lift, and you shouldn't shy away from the idea of pampering yourself at this time.

If you cannot alleviate the depression by yourself, then you should see your doctor who will either recommend counselling or anti-depressant drugs. These can be a great help, and your doctor will prescribe the most suitable for you.

Counselling

This may be the answer to your anxiety or depression as well as helping you over difficulties both physical and emotional in your relationships. A trained counsellor will give you a lot of help and support. Ask your doctor to suggest whom you may go to for counselling, or try one of the agencies listed at the end of this book. A trained counsellor may be a psychologist, a psychiatric social worker, a clergyman, your doctor, or even your doctor's practice nurse.

Alternatively your doctor may put you in touch with a health visitor or community health worker who will come and talk to you about your worries. This is a very useful system, as the health visitor's care and advice can be tied in with any medical treatment you are receiving.

Marion, a kindly forty-nine year old, lived in a council house with her husband and five children. She was worried because she kept getting a feeling that her heart was beating violently. She had tingling in her fingers and a few hot flushes; her periods had stopped the year before and she wondered if her symptoms could be due to the menopause. I examined her and we carried out an electrocardiogram test, which ruled out heart disease. Then Marion started to tell me her problems and I realized that she was suffering from anxiety.

Marion's situation at home was very difficult. Her husband and eldest son were on the dole and the youngest boy had been in trouble with the police for stealing. The family also owed a lot of money for hire-purchase on the furniture.

Release of adrenaline was causing Marion's heart to beat more strongly and her nervous panting and over-breathing resulted in changes in the acidity of the blood, which caused tingling in the hands and feet.

I asked a health visitor to see her, and she helped both Marion and her family deal with their problems. Gradually her state of anxiety subsided.

Resuming or taking up a full time job will provide plenty of new interest.

Your career

The menopause can be a good time to take stock of your career prospects. If your children are leaving home you will have more time on your hands. If you have continued to work from the time you finished your education, your routine will be unaltered at least in this respect, and during this period when so much else is changing in your life, an anchor of that sort can be a tremendous help. You will be able to devote more energy to your job and probably find a rewarding satisfaction in that.

On the other hand, perhaps you started a career, or training, but gave it up when you had a family. You could make enquiries about taking a refresher course or completing your original training programme.

Embarking on a career will open up a whole new life to you and your network of relationships will be expanded to include lots of new friends. You will be so busy taking in all kinds of impressions, absorbing information and getting to know people, that you may find the menopause has passed almost unnoticed.

Indian women who are kept in strict seclusion (purdah) experience a great release at the time of the menopause, because custom then allows them to travel about freely and to talk and drink in male company. They are so delighted with their freedom and their new, active role in life that they experience none of the unpleasant menopausal symptoms. This remarkable fact seems to indicate that the fuller your life, the less chance you have of being bothered by the menopause.

Whatever lifestyle you opt for in your middle years, you will want to keep up your confidence and self-esteem, and to do this one of your prime aims will be to stay fit and healthy and youthful-looking. In the next chapter I tell you the best ways to maintain good health.

4 STAYING YOUNG AND HEALTHY

There isn't a magic formula for staying young and healthy for ever, but there is a lot you can do to retain your youth and vitality well past the time of the menopause. There is no reason to think your looks will fade just because you have reached the menopause. You can go on feeling lively and young and be as sexually attractive as you want, so long as you take care of your health. Many women think that hormone treatment is the only answer, and there is no doubt that this can be of help in certain cases (see Chapter 6), but there are other measures you can take yourself that can be as beneficial as any drugs.

You will need to watch your weight and to know which foods to cut down on to lessen the chance of heart disease. Learning about osteoporosis (see Chapter 1) will have made you realize the importance of calcium, the bone-building mineral, in your diet. You should think seriously about smoking and its adverse effects on your health, and if possible try to give it up. You should take enough physical exercise – and mental exercise too! At this time of life it is quite normal to sleep less, so lack of sleep need not worry you. Use the time gained to do the things that you enjoy and that interest you most.

Putting on weight

Even if you have never had a weight problem before you may now find that you have put on several pounds and an extra inch or so around the middle. Glandular changes can make some people gain weight at the menopause but the commonest cause is eating and drinking more than you need. Women burn up calories more slowly than men and your energy requirement falls as you grow older. You are no longer rushing around after the children and if you are sitting down all day your energy needs could be half what they used to be.

Even if you put on only a little weight you will find it harder to get up out of a chair, and you may find that you are doing less and walking more slowly so that a vicious circle is set up of less exercise, making you gain more. About 30 lb (14 kg) over your ideal weight can put a lot of pressure on your lower spine, hips and knees so that they may become painful; then you move more carefully still and put on even more weight.

Weight with shoes and indoor clothes

Ht ins	Ht cms	Wt (lb) small build	Kg	Medium build (lb)	Kg	Large build (lb)	Kg
4 11	149·9	108	49·0	117	53·1	129	58·5
5 0	152·4	109	49·4	120	54·4	132	59·9
5 1	154·9	114	51·7	123	55·8	135	61·2
5 2	157·5	117	53·1	127	57·6	139	63·0
5 3	160·0	120	54·4	131	59·4	143	64·9
5 4	162·6	124	56·2	136	61·7	147	66·7
5 5	165·1	128	58·1	140	63·5	151	68·5
5 6	167·6	132	59·9	144	65·3	155	70·3
5 7	170·2	136	61·7	148	67·1	159	72·1
5 8	172·7	141	64·0	152	68·9	164	74·4
5 9	175·3	145	65·8	156	70·8	169	76·7
5 10	177·8	149	67·6	160	72·6	175	79·4

Table of average weights for women at the menopause.

If you are too heavy, try to slim until you are as near as possible to your ideal weight. If you need to lose more than 7 lb (3 kg), try following a balanced 1000 calorie diet to reduce your daily intake. Do not go on a crash starvation diet. You won't be able to keep to it and once you give it up you will quickly put on weight again as your metabolic rate will have changed and be unable to cope with a normal quantity. Slimming tablets are not really the answer either, and sometimes they can be dangerous. But it is a good idea to join a slimming club where you can compare notes with other people aiming at the same goal. If in doubt about what you should be aiming for and how best to achieve it, always consult your doctor.

Follow a healthy eating pattern
Weight-watchers are not the only people who should be conscious of their diet. Whether you are trying to slim or not you should avoid eating certain foods all the more carefully as you approach the middle years:

1. Avoid fatty foods, which are associated with the onset of heart disease.
2. Reduce your intake of salt to lessen the likelihood of high blood pressure.
3. Increase your intake of fibre which protects against these and other diseases such as diabetes and some types of cancer.

Here are a few guidelines on what are the wrong and right foods for a healthy diet:

- Reduce the amount of refined sugar you eat in sweets and cakes or take in drinks.
- Eat less red meat: even lean meat contains fat between the muscle fibres.
- Try eating more fish, or choose chicken or turkey, as both are less fatty than other meats, especially when you don't eat the skin.
- Cut down on eggs – one or two a week is ideal.
- Where you can, avoid sausages, including salami and black pudding, pâté, pies, suet pudding, butter, cream, cream cheese, bacon and ham, as all contain a lot of saturated animal fat.
- It is better to eat fresh foods than manufactured or packaged products, which often contain extra salt.
- Do eat plenty of fresh fruit and vegetables. These contain valuable vitamins as well as being cheap.
- Use sunflower seed or corn oil for cooking and polyunsaturated margarine on bread.
- Try leaving the peel on potatoes and apples for the added fibre.
- Use wholemeal flour for baking; the bran in it will increase your fibre intake.
- Drink water rather than the diuretics tea or coffee, especially in hot weather when you lose water by evaporation and sweating.
- Eat fibre-rich breakfast cereals, home-made muesli or oatmeal porridge.
- Valuable protein is contained in wholemeal bread, wheatgerm, oats, peas, beans and lentils, so the more you eat of these, the less meat you will need.

This advice applies to your partner too, for he will also be at greater risk of developing heart disease or high blood pressure. If you adopt a healthy eating pattern together it will be easier to follow for you both and you will certainly enjoy the benefits more if you can share them.

The importance of fibre
Foods containing fibre include those in the last two categories listed above, as well as fresh vegetables such as spinach, potatoes, cabbage and the pulses. Miller's bran, which you can take sprinkled on your breakfast cereal, is the highest source of fibre.

The reason for increasing your fibre intake is that it absorbs water and contributes to the growth of beneficial bacteria in your gut. This process makes a bulky stool, providing exercise for the bowel, so keeping your intestine in healthy working order and reducing the risks of bowel disease. Dr Denis Burkitt's book *Don't Forget Fibre in your Diet (Eat Right to Stay Healthy)* in this series explains the latest finding on the importance of fibre as a protection against many diseases we in the West are susceptible to, particularly from the middle years.

Alcohol

Heavy drinking is not good for you. Everyone knows the dangers of alcoholism, and it is from regular drinking in large quantities that alcoholism can develop. It is easy to fall into a dependence on alcohol if you are going through a depressed period, but you will not in the end solve your problems with drink and you may cause a lot of unhappiness in your family.

It is now believed that a small intake of alcohol, about a glass of wine or half a pint of beer a day, may reduce the risk of heart disease by helping you relax and avoid habitual tension and anxiety. But don't forget that alcohol is high in calories, so slimmers should beware.

Avoiding osteoporosis

After the menopause there is an increased risk of osteoporosis (see Chapter 1). A survey has shown that bone density in women reaches its peak at thirty-five to forty and then declines steadily. It was found that when this decline starts the jaw bones are very often affected, causing teeth to loosen and fall out. However, a calcium supplement in the diet prevented further bone loss. Calcium supplements plus hormone therapy were found to be the most effective form of treatment, and even led to increased bone thickness in some people.

If you start taking extra calcium in your diet around the time of the menopause, you should avoid early signs of osteoporosis and may not need hormone therapy. You should have 1500 mg of calcium every day after the menopause, and the table opposite shows you how to achieve this with a balanced intake of calcium-rich foods. Don't forget the advice about controlling the quantity of fat in your diet; calcium can and should be taken in other forms besides milk and cheese.

If you don't reach 1500 mg calcium every day, even a small amount is better than none and will help protect your bones.

If you are already having any medical treatment, you should ask your doctor whether it has an effect on your calcium balance. If you have hypercalcaemia, a very rare condition, it may not be safe to take calcium supplements.

Other ways of maintaining strong bones

- As thinning of the bones occurs mostly while you are lying in bed, try to get up a bit earlier.
- Exercise strengthens bone, so aim to take regular exercise in the form of walking or a favourite sport (see below too).
- Take moderate amounts of sunshine, as it forms vitamin D in the skin and helps your intestine to absorb calcium. (Too much will of course have an ageing effect on your skin, so be sensible about sunbathing.)
- Have a dental check at least once a year. This should preserve a set of healthy teeth and keep your face looking youthful.

Ways of increasing calcium intake

Daily requirement before menopause	1000 mg
after menopause	1500 mg

Calcium content of pills available over the counter

	Pills providing 600 mg
Calcium gluconate 600 mg contains 54 mg calcium	12
Calcium lactate 300 mg contains 44 mg calcium	14
Sandocal − 4.5 g contains 400 mg calcium	1½

Calcium content of common foods in mg per 100 g (3½ oz approx) of food

Dairy	mg
Cheese	
Cheddar	800
Cottage (low fat soft cheese)	60
Danish Blue	580
Edam	740
Parmesan	1220
processed	700
spread	510
Cream	79
Egg (whole)	52
Egg (yolk)	130
Milk (3.53 fl oz/98 ml)	120
Yoghurt − low fat (5 oz/145 ml)	180

Meat and fish

Meat contains very small amounts of calcium, as does fish. Meat pies and fish in batter contain calcium in the flour. Canned pilchards and sardines, sprats and whitebait contain calcium in the bones.

Boiled prawns	150
Canned crab	120
pilchards	300
salmon	93
sardines	460–550
Fried sprats	620–710
whitebait	860
Fish paste	280
Steamed scallops	120

Vegetables	
Beans, haricot (navy)	180
kidney	140
Broccoli	100
Cabbage	53
Chick peas (garbanzos)	140
Greens, turnip, cale, collard, mustard	98
Olives in brine	61
Parsley	330
Peas (boiled/frozen)	31
Spinach (boiled)	600
Spring onions (scallions)	140
Watercress	220

Fruit	mg
Apricots, dried	92
Blackcurrants, raw	60
Currants, dried	95
Figs, dried	280
Lemon, whole	110
Rhubarb, raw	100

Nuts (shelled weight)	
Almonds	250
Barcelonas	170
Brazils	180
Peanuts (groundnuts), roasted and salted	61
Sesame seeds	870

Drinks (dry weight)	
Cocoa powder	130
Coffee, ground	130
instant	160
Malted milk drink (Horlicks)	230
Tea, Indian	430

Cooking ingredients	
Baking powder (depending on brand)	11300
Curry powder	640
Mustard, dry	330
Pepper	130
Salt, block	230
Stock cubes (depending on brand)	180
Yeast, dried	80

Flour and baked foods	
Bread (white or brown)	100
Hovis (UK)	150
Cake, sponge (fatless)	140
rock (individual fruit cakes)	390
Flour, plain (cake)	130
self-raising	350
Soya flour	210–40
Wheat bran	110

Smoking

Please stop smoking. There is such a big risk to your health from heavy smoking that it is neglectful to go on with it. The hormonal changes after the menopause double the risk of you having a heart attack, and if you smoke forty cigarettes a day the risk is doubled again. The likelihood of many diseases, such as heart attacks, lung cancer, stomach ulcers and cancer of the pancreas or bladder is increased by smoking in proportion to the number of cigarettes that you get through each day. Even low tar cigarettes carry a significant risk.

If you smoke heavily you are more likely to have an early menopause than if you do not smoke at all. The reason for this is as yet unknown, but it is thought that smoking affects the pituitary gland and causes premature ageing.

One of the reasons why women go on smoking is that they sometimes gain weight when they stop. The best solution is to tackle both problems at once, your smoking habit and the tendency to put on weight. This is not as odd or as difficult as it may seem. The anxious woman who reaches for a cigarette to relieve tensions often eats for comfort as an alternative.

How you stop compulsive smoking and eating will depend on you. Hypnosis, acupuncture, self-help groups, tranquillizers, relaxation therapy or just sheer willpower all work as long as you are determined to break the habit.

Exercise

We take exercise all the time, even when we are asleep in bed, but the amount depends on the sort of people we are. A jumpy person who sits on the edge of a chair, throws her arms and legs about and rushes around everywhere seems to be able to eat anything without getting fat. Her opposite number sits quietly and moves around slowly, perhaps wearing high heels that stop her walking fast, and she prefers taking a car or an elevator to walking. When she is sleeping she lies almost still in bed instead of moving her limbs about when she is dreaming. It is not surprising that she puts on weight as she is burning up only a fraction of the calories she eats.

Try to take plenty of exercise. Sex is good for you, so are walking, cycling, swimming and any other sport or activity you enjoy. Exercise protects the heart, lowers the blood pressure and greatly reduces your chances of getting stiff joints or problems with the circulation. Just take care over one or two points:

- If you are only beginning an exercise programme now, start gently and build up gradually as your level of fitness increases. If you go overboard with violent exercise before you're ready you may strain your heart. Walking and swimming are safe forms of exercise; jogging, squash or aerobics are for people who are already fit. You should get advice from your doctor if you're not sure whether you can manage these sports.

- If you do go jogging, wear first-class training shoes. Otherwise the shock of impact can damage your weight-bearing joints. Fast walking is kinder to your feet.
- Take exercise regularly. Make a habit of walking or running upstairs instead of using the elevator. If you can manage twenty minutes' exercise that makes you breathless three times a week this will do you more good than a marathon run at the weekend with no exercise in between.
- It is easy to do a few exercises while you are in the bath; lying back and pedalling an imaginary bike with your feet in the air improves the circulation. A good brisk rub with a towel afterwards, all over the body including your head, tones your skin and feels wonderful.
- Exercises that involve rapid spinal movements may lead to a painful back so it is better to stick to the exercises where you keep your back straight and bend your knees instead. Heavy weights can also strain your back. If you are carrying a heavy load divide it into two when possible so that you are doing more walking and less weight-lifting.
- Mental exercise is just as important as physical exercise, and a lively and well-informed mind can keep you young well into old age. Keep up with current affairs, read books on subjects that interest you and go to the cinema and theatre when you can.

How much sleep do you need?

If you find that sleep doesn't come as easily as it used to, don't lie awake worrying about it! Many people find that their sleeping pattern changes as they grow older and they may only need five or six instead of eight hours a night.

Two studies that took place in California looked at the sleep requirements of ten subjects who normally slept eight hours every night. Their nightly sleep was cut by half an hour every three weeks. They found that they were able to function perfectly well in the daytime without feeling too sleepy until they had cut down to five hours' sleep at night. There was no reduction in the amount of deep sleep that they experienced. A year later nearly all of them had maintained the reduction of sleeping time – about one to two and a half hours less than the original eight hours – and they felt well and alert.

How can you get a better night's sleep? Sleeping tablets can make you feel muzzy-headed next day, although some preparations are better than others in this respect. Most of them cause a reduction in the amount of rapid eye movement (REM) sleep, in which dreams occur, and this is not necessarily a good thing; it is widely believed that fears and conflicts are acted out during dreams, providing a natural safety valve for anxiety. When people stop taking sleeping pills, they experience extra REM sleep, almost as if they are trying to make up for the amount lost. Instead of asking for sleeping pills you may find that you can adapt your rhythm to a shorter night, perhaps compensating with a nap during the day.

If you decide to cut down your sleeping time as a remedy for sleeplessness you will need to think of some occupation for those quiet hours during the night. Reading, knitting and needlework are all soothing pastimes.

Natural sleep without pills is the best way of restoring health to your psyche. If, however, you are lying awake night after night feeling desperately deprived of sleep it is safe to take half a pill occasionally, as this will not start a habit of dependence. It is better to have pills for this purpose prescribed by your doctor, who knows what type you will be suited to, than to buy them directly over the counter.

A very common cause of disturbed sleep is depression, which may not be obvious to you, so that your main difficulty is waking early in the morning and feeling tired during the day. If you think you have this problem see your doctor about it, as the most effective treatment is not sleeping tablets but anti-depressants (see also Chapter 3).

Medical check-ups

Around the time of the menopause it is common sense to arrange for your doctor to give you a brief medical check. This will include measurement of your height, weight and blood pressure, examination of the breasts and pelvis, a urine test, a cervical smear test and a discussion of any problems or symptoms that are bothering you (I describe these tests in more detail in Chapter 5). The information will provide useful data for your doctor if you are ill at some time in the future.

Examining your breasts You should in any case examine your breasts yourself just once a month. This will ensure that any little lump that develops is noticed early on and you can then see your doctor about it. If you are still having periods the best time is immediately after the period as then the breasts are smaller and less lumpy.

1. Sit in front of a mirror and look carefully for any signs of changing shape or size in either breast (though remember that many women have one breast larger than the other all their lives) – or signs of soreness or swelling on the skin.

2. With your hands on your hips, squeeze your tummy in so your breasts lift. Look again for any change in shape.
3. Lie flat on your back and examine each breast in turn. Using two fingers of the opposite hand to the breast being examined, make very slow, circular movements, moving from the outside inwards until you have checked the whole breast.
4. If you have large breasts, make this check with a pillow underneath the shoulder of the breast to be examined so that the breast is extended and easier to check.

There is no need to *expect* trouble with your breasts during the menopause but it is as important to check them like this as it is to maintain fitness in the other ways I have described in this chapter. Taking an active role in looking after your health will encourage you to keep to your good intentions.

In the next chapter I give some advice on when and why you may need to see your doctor, and the sort of examinations you will have.

5 SEEING YOUR DOCTOR

The main symptoms of the menopause and the ways to cope with them I have already described. Here I examine other problems not directly associated with the menopause, but which may occur at the same time. These need a doctor's diagnosis and treatment, and you should not hesitate to go for examination if you are worried about your health.

Doctors often have great difficulty in making an accurate diagnosis because of the worries of their patients. Some, as was the case with Lilian (page 18), may believe that they have something seriously wrong with them when they are just experiencing the normal effects of the menopause; others blame the menopause when they have some other trouble.

Alice, a vivacious blonde of forty-five, had become more and more tired. She had a few flushes and came to see me to ask if she could start hormone therapy. When I examined her I found she had large fibroids (see page 16) and she then told me that she had heavy periods; a blood count showed that she was anaemic. She was treated successfully with iron tablets as well as having the fibroids removed. The cause of the tiredness was not the menopause but anaemia.

Alice has remained very well without any hormone treatment. But I shall be happy to give her hormone replacement therapy if she needs it later.

When should you see your doctor?

Women often come to see me with aches and pains, saying that these are due to the menopause. They are not. However, if you are bothered by anything that stops you doing all you want, do see your doctor. Pains in the chest may be caused by stress and anxiety, but they can be a symptom of heart disease. The earlier your doctor makes a diagnosis the more effective the treatment will be.

Coronary heart disease is much rarer in women than in men, and the incidence does not become equal in the sexes until the age of seventy. The indications are that oestrogen protects against heart disease, while male hormones increase the likelihood of it occurring.

You are quite likely to get minor aches and pains during the middle years, brought on by too much exertion, or perhaps too little. Aching joints are not the same as osteoporosis but they are helped by gentle exercise, warmth, attention to the height of chairs and a comfortable warm bed. You should not carry heavy weights. If the pain gets bad and you can't for the moment see your doctor aspirin or paracetamol can bring relief. It is best to use aspirin in the soluble or coated form, which is less of an irritant to the stomach.

What your doctor needs to know

Most of the information the doctor needs to make a diagnosis comes from what you say about yourself. So it is important that you should think out carefully what is the chief thing that is troubling you and give a clear story of when it started, how bad it is and whether you have had it previously. If you give an accurate history your doctor will probably be able to make a mental list of things that might be wrong before examining you. There are some that may be hard to talk about, such as sexual difficulty or the fact that your partner is ill. Do try to be honest as it makes the job of helping you much easier. Here are a few points to bear in mind when you visit your doctor.

1. It is useful to write down the dates of your periods to see whether they are regular. 'It was due last Tuesday but one but it was three days late' is the sort of description doctors find hard to disentangle.
2. Your doctor needs to know which method of contraception you are using and whether you suspect you are pregnant.
3. Information about any operations and major diseases you have had and their treatment is important. Your family may have a tendency to certain diseases and you should mention this too.

What tests will you have?

There are a number of tests your doctor will make according to the symptoms you describe. Often the preliminary part of your examination is carried out by a nurse – the measurement of your height, weight and blood pressure.

Pelvic examination   This is the main part of any examination by your doctor, and it will reveal whether you have any of the troubles I describe in this chapter.

You will need to empty your bladder before the doctor examines your pelvis, but bear in mind that you may be asked for a urine sample. The best plan is not to go to the toilet until you have told the doctor your symptoms. Then he or she will ask you to empty your bladder and give a sample at the same time if necessary.

For an examination of the pelvis, you will have to take off the lower half of your clothes. Try to avoid having a bath or a douche or using pessaries or talc beforehand, as these may hide any symptoms you might have and make a diagnosis more difficult. The doctor may get you to lie on your side with legs tucked up, or on your back with your legs bent and apart.

Sometimes a swab of vaginal discharge is taken. This is painless and is done by touching the top of the vagina with a cottonwool bud on a stick, which is then inserted into a tube where the bacteria can grow.

The cervical smear Many doctors arrange for periodic screening of women over thirty-five for cervical cancer by taking a smear test at regular intervals every three to five years until the age of sixty-five (in North America often once a year). If you have had two negative smears, you can usually stop at this age. It is not necessary to have more frequent tests unless you have at any time had an abnormal result, or you have noticed a symptom such as irregular bleeding.

The doctor will put on a disposable glove and insert a speculum, which is a hinged piece of metal, into the vagina. When the hinge opens, the doctor can see the cervix or neck of the womb protruding into the vagina. A smear is taken by rotating a wooden spatula round the cervix to pick up a layer of cells. It is smeared on to a glass slide and then squirted with alcohol fixative. The slide is usually sent to a laboratory for staining and examination under a microscope.

Vaginal smear This gives information about the level of oestrogen in your blood. The doctor takes a smear from the upper part of the vagina, which is treated in the same way as a cervical smear. Then he or she inserts two fingers into the vagina to feel the womb and the tubes and to check whether there is any enlargement of the ovaries. At the same time as the smear the doctor may give you a more thorough check:

Your rectum or back passage may also be examined, and this is usually done while you are lying on your left side.

Your abdomen The doctor examines your abdomen with the flat of the hand.

Examining your breasts The doctor will probably also examine your breasts, although this is a check that you should be making regularly yourself. The best time is monthly, after each period (see Chapter 4).

If you have noticed a lump do say exactly where it is as a tiny one may easily go unnoticed. Usually a significant lump in the breast feels like a dried pea or bean but it can be larger. The size is no indication of whether or not the lump is malignant.

Should your mother or sister have had breast cancer it may be possible for you to be screened every year in addition to checking your breasts yourself every month.

Further examination If the doctor has found anything unusual, further tests may be necessary. A blood sample may be taken to check whether you are anaemic. You may be referred to a gynaecologist for an examination of the lining of the womb. This is called a D and C, short for dilatation and curettage (see Chapter 7). It is carried out under an anaesthetic, which enables the gynaecologist to make a further examination of your womb and ovaries.

Some centres also offer a special 'soft' X-ray of the breasts (mammography) and a check on the temperature of the breast tissue (thermography). None of these tests is either painful or frightening.

Diagnosis

The doctor may diagnose your complaint immediately, or it may be necessary to wait for the results of your tests. Taking a swab of vaginal discharge should suggest whether you have any of the following conditions:

- TV (trichomonas vaginitis)
- Thrush
- Venereal disease.

A slight urinary incontinence may be caused by a prolapse of the womb or cystitis.

None of these conditions is necessarily to be expected at the menopause, but all are quite common. Women are more vulnerable to infection after the menopause because the lining of the vagina has grown thinner.

Vaginal discharge

This is one of those problems that a woman can suffer from at any age, and in fact most women get it at one time or another. It does not usually indicate anything serious, neither is it due to poor standards of hygiene. Blood-stained discharge is common around the menopause as a result of changes in your hormone balance (see Chapter 1). This or irregular spotting should always be reported to your doctor, who can make sure that you do not have cancer. *Don't* put off a visit: the earlier a diagnosis is made the sooner you can have effective treatment.

Some discharge is just due to natural causes, like the secretion that occurs when you ovulate. If you have been on oral contraceptives until the age of forty you may be surprised at the amount of discharge that appears when you ovulate for the first time after stopping the Pill. This needn't worry you at all. In fact, the more natural discharge you have the easier and therefore more enjoyable sex is.

The conditions I describe below are the commonest types of infected discharge that women get around the menopause. The drying up of vaginal secretions makes you more vulnerable to picking up infections and this can happen in various ways: from going with a new partner, from using an unhygienic lavatory seat, or someone else's dirty towel.

Whatever you do, don't try and clear up your problem on your own and don't use harsh cleansers when you are sore. One of the most common disorders I see in the surgery is the effect of women doing just that. They buy a bottle of strong disinfectant, slop it into the bath and give themselves a douche. Not surprisingly, this makes the delicate membranes very sore and red.

Bath salts can be too alkaline and destroy the surface cells of the vagina. Bubble baths can have a similar effect. Some women scour the bath with a detergent or cleaning powder and then run the bath and bathe in the diluted detergent to prevent a rim of scum forming. When I examine them I find two problems, the original discharge plus the horrid effects of self-treatment. The ways the discharges should be treated I describe below.

Trichomonas vaginitis (TV)

This produces a bubbly yellow discharge that stains the pants brown and is worse after a period. Although it doesn't cause much itching, it can be smelly. It is treated with a week's course of metronidazole tablets or pessaries, or sometimes both are given together. Avoid alcohol during treatment or you may feel sick and dizzy.

Although TV is naturally occurring, you can pass it to your partner, who can in turn give it back to you, so that you never get rid of it even though the treatment is effective. Because of this, your partner should also be checked for TV, and if he has it make sure he is treated too.

Thrush

This produces a thick white discharge that looks like bits of milk curd or yoghurt. It is a common condition. In one doctor's practice 48 per cent of women with white discharge were found to have thrush. It is not a serious infection but it is very itchy and can make you sore. The treatment is a course of nystatin pessaries or other fungicidal treatment which can itself produce a yellow discharge. Cream containing nystatin together with steroids to reduce itch and inflammation is also used.

As with TV, your partner may need treatment too, to stop re-infection. He can be given nystatin cream to put under the foreskin. You should carry on using this cream when you have sex until you are both sure the thrush has cleared up.

Itch of the vulva or anus

The vulva is the fleshy area around the vagina and urethra and itchiness there and around the anus is a common problem. It is called pruritus and can be a great nuisance, keeping you awake at night. Usually pruritus is caused by thrush, when it is treated as above. But it may be due to vaginal deodorants or sprays, and will clear up if you avoid them and take a daily bath in clean water. Another cause can be an allergy to contraceptive sheaths or cream, in which case you can change your contraceptive.

If the discomfort hasn't cleared after a week, see your doctor who will suggest which are the best applications for you to try, and if necessary will give you a course of anti-histamine pills or hydrocortisone cream to calm the itchiness. He or she may check your urine for sugar as diabetes can cause pruritus.

Scabies or crab lice

These infections, often caught from a sexual partner, can also produce a nasty itch. If you rub the skin a lot it gets thick and red; and sometimes the whole area around the upper thighs is affected. Your doctor will prescribe a lotion which will rid you of the soreness in a few days.

Venereal disease

Sexually transmitted diseases (STD) are not uncommon around the time of the menopause. A woman may launch out into a sexual adventure or her partner may have an affair and infect her.

If you have a sudden increase in the amount of discharge and particularly if it is yellow or blood-stained and you suspect you have VD, you should report it at once. Special STD or VD clinics are extremely competent at dealing with this problem and have better facilities for diagnosis than the average family doctor. They also try to prevent disease spreading to the sexual partner.

I sometimes feel saddened at the reluctance of many people to attend these clinics, which in the UK offer a first-class service free of charge. You should overcome your scruples and be frank about your problem. The doctor is there to help you, not to judge you. Venereal disease will not simply go away and if it is allowed to spread unchecked it may travel up into the uterus and tubes and cause severe pain and abscesses.

Prolapse

Prolapse simply means something coming down. Because the supports of the womb and vagina are weakened after childbirth the womb hangs further down into the passage. A loose pouch of vaginal skin may bulge out, with the bladder attached (like a double chin at the lower end of the body) – this is a cystocele. A rectocele is a similar pouch at the back of the vagina into which the rectum bulges. These harmless swellings can sometimes be felt in the vagina if you bear down. The main problem is that a cystocele is often associated with involuntary passing of urine (stress incontinence). This can be a serious social problem as you may find that you wet your pants if you laugh or sneeze or exert yourself. The weakening of the supports stretches the ring of muscle at the outlet of the bladder and so you are unable to prevent urine spurting out when pressure increases.

There are some useful exercises that you can do (see diagram overleaf).

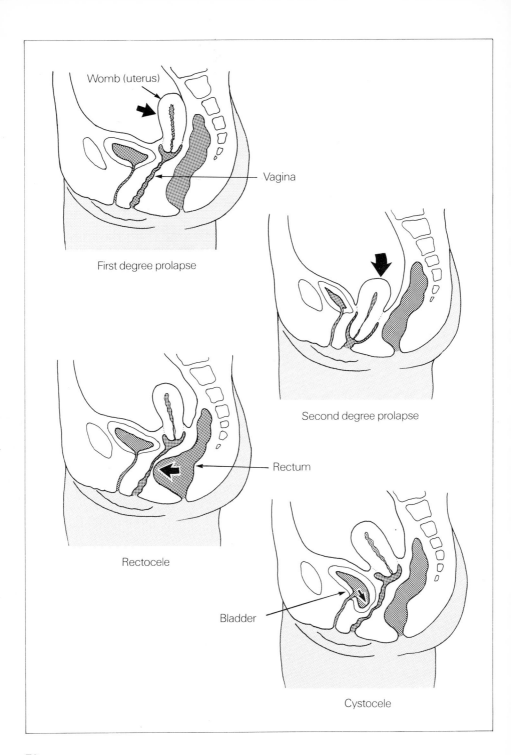

Womb (uterus)

Vagina

First degree prolapse

Second degree prolapse

Rectum

Rectocele

Bladder

Cystocele

To help a prolapse

1. Stand with your legs apart and insert two fingers into the vagina (see opposite). Contract the muscles in your pelvis to squeeze your fingers. Do not move your legs. You may feel the back passage lift up and away from your fingers. The muscle you use is called the levator ani (lifter of the anus).
2. Practise holding in your urine or holding back a motion. This can be done at any time, when you remember.

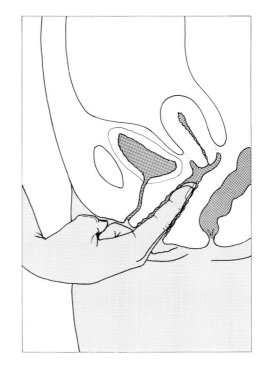

(*Above*) Exercises to help a prolapse

(*Left*) The different types and degrees of prolapse

It is also helpful when you go out to insert a lubricated tampon into the vagina to support the bladder.

If these measures do not help you may need an operation to hitch the loose skin into place again and tighten up the muscles (see Chapter 7).

Cystitis
After the menopause the vaginal tissues and the base of the bladder are more fragile and easily bruised. On the day after intercourse it is not uncommon to get an attack of cystitis. You want to pass water very frequently, and feel a soreness and a burning sensation whenever you try.

To prevent this, remember to empty your bladder before and after sex. You can also use a vaginal lubricant such as K-Y jelly, which should help reduce the amount of damage at the base of the bladder (see also Chapter 1, Dryness of the vagina).

Will you need further treatment?
The vaginal troubles I describe in this chapter are usually cleared up easily and there is no need for further investigation or specialist treatment. But your doctor may decide to get a gynaecologist's opinion for a condition

that persists even with the usual treatment. After your visit the specialist will write to your own doctor with details of the treatment that you require. Go back and see your doctor as soon as he or she has this letter so that you can get the prescribed medical treatment. You may be told that you are going to need an operation (the sort of operation you may have I describe in Chapter 7) but there is no need for you to be worried before going into hospital that you won't know what is going to be done. Ask your doctor to tell you exactly what is going to happen and what the effects will be.

I have mentioned hormone replacement therapy in several chapters already. This form of treatment can be very effective for relieving various troubles of the menopause. If your doctor is considering giving you hormone therapy, he or she may arrange for an examination of the lining of your womb before you start treatment. I explain exactly what hormone therapy is, and its benefits, in the next chapter.

6 HORMONE REPLACEMENT THERAPY

Hormone treatment of menopausal women has been widely used in the United States for over thirty years, and in 1975 it was estimated that ten million American women were receiving it. When publicity about hormone replacement therapy (HRT) reached the United Kingdom in 1973, it raised great expectations among many women that it would keep them young, active and beautiful for a long time after the menopause. But it has not caught on in the UK as expected and at present only 2 per cent of menopausal women – just 160,000 – use it.

What is HRT?
Hormone replacement therapy is the name for a course of the female hormones, oestrogen and progestogen. The aim in increasing the supply of hormones at the time of the menopause and afterwards is to reduce or postpone some of the uncomfortable physical effects I described in Chapter 1. Your hormone balance is kept at pre-menopausal level so you continue to feel fit and healthy, although you no longer have a true cycle, with ovulation.

Is HRT right for you?
There is no doubt that in some cases HRT is enormously beneficial. Basically, it helps three types of women:

- Those suffering from hot flushes, or flashes
- from osteoporosis
- or from vaginal dryness, atrophy and urinary problems (these last occur in the later post-menopausal period).

There is no evidence that HRT actually improves your looks or figure, but of course if you *feel* better, you tend to look better too.

However, HRT is only one of the treatments that can be used to help you at the menopause, and it may not always be the best choice in your particular situation. Not all women benefit from extra hormones – overweight women, for example, manufacture more oestrogen in their bodies than others do. About one-fifth experience no symptoms of the menopause at all, and many others are not enthusiastic about long-term treatment. A pattern of plenty of the right kind of food, exercise, sleep and sunshine is right for most women.

When will HRT be recommended for you?

Suppose that you are about fifty-two years old, your periods are very irregular and you are feeling tired and getting hot flushes. You go to see your doctor and explain your symptoms. The doctor examines you, checks your breasts and blood pressure and takes a blood test that shows you are not anaemic and your thyroid gland is working normally. The doctor arranges for you to have a D and C (see Chapter 7) to make sure that you have no underlying condition and that your womb is normal. When the doctor is satisfied with the results, and provided that you have not had a major disease such as cancer of the breast or thrombosis, HRT can be prescribed.

Which preparation?

If you have a womb (that is, you have not had a hysterectomy), you will need a combined hormone preparation containing oestrogen and progestogen (artificially manufactured progesterone). Treatment was originally given with oestrogen alone, but this caused overgrowth of the lining of the womb, which can lead to cancer. Progestogen helps to prevent cancer by protecting the lining of the womb from over-stimulation – indeed it is sometimes used to treat cancer of the womb.

Taking the combined menopausal pill is a bit like taking the contraceptive Pill, but the doses are much lower. It does mean that you will have regular 'periods'. They are not, of course, true periods, which are triggered off by ovulation. In one popular preparation the pills for the first eleven days contain oestrogen alone. Those for the next ten days contain oestrogen plus progestogen. When the second set are finished there is a break for seven days and bleeding occurs as the lining of the womb is shed. This is the 'period' – it does not mean you are fertile. The 'cycle' is now complete and you are ready to start the next. These pills are not strong enough to be contraceptive so you still need to use contraception if you are under fifty-five.

Each preparation is a little different. One of them contains oestrogen in small doses, to be taken in the last seven days, when you have a period. If your doctor says that oestrogen is not suitable for you, it may be possible for you to take progestogen alone. Recent research by Dr Lorraine Dennerstein of the University of Melbourne, Australia, and Prof Robert Lindsay and Dr David McKay Hart in Glasgow, Scotland, working independently, has shown that progestogens have a good effect on menopausal symptoms and thinning of the bones – even if the results are not quite as good as with oestrogens.

How do you know if you have reached the menopause?   If you started HRT before your periods stopped you won't know when you have reached the true menopause. The only way to find out is to come off HRT and see if your periods go on afterwards.

Hormone replacements used at the menopause

Drug		Daily dose
Oestrogens	ethinyl oestradiol	10–50 micrograms daily, reducing to 10 or 20
	oestriol (Ovestin)	250–500 micrograms daily
	conjugated oestrogens (Premarin)	0.625–1.25 mg daily
	oestrone (Harmogen)	1.5–4.5 mg daily
	quinestradol (Pentovis)	250–500 micrograms daily
	Hormonin	½–2 tablets daily
Progestogens	dydrogesterone (Duphaston)	10 mg twice daily, 11th–25th day of cycle
	medroxyprogesterone (Provera)	5 mg daily, 16th–21st day of cycle
	norethisterone (Primolut N) (Utovlan)	5 mg 3 times daily to stop bleeding; 5 mg twice daily, 19th–26th day, to prevent bleeding
Combined preparations containing oestrogen and progestogen	Cyclo-Progynova	1 mg or 2 mg for 21 days, then 7 days' interval
	Menophase	Take in sequence without interruption
	Prempak–C	0.625 mg or 1.25 mg, take in sequence without interruption
	Trisequens	Take in sequence without interruption
Oestrogen and testosterone	Mixogen	1–2 tablets daily for 3 weeks
Implants	oestradiol testosterone	25 or 50 or 100 mg about every 36 weeks; variable dosage

Note: For equivalent international drug names, see tables on page 102

How often should you see your doctor?

Your doctor will arrange to see you soon after you begin treatment to see if it is suiting you. Thereafter you will be examined periodically, and you should check your breasts yourself each month after the 'period' (see Chapter 4).

Every two years you may need to see a gynaecologist for a D and C or endometrial biopsy to check that the lining of your womb is still normal. If you notice irregular bleeding you should see the gynaecologist as soon as possible for this test.

Hysterectomy and HRT

Of course, if you have had a hysterectomy, you will not need a D and C. In our practice, the great majority of patients on HRT are those who have had the womb removed. For them supervision is quick and easy and can be carried out by the family doctor. After hysterectomy you do not need progestogen to prevent you getting cancer of the womb, because of course you have no womb. So is it is quite safe to use oestrogen alone. You can take it all the time, and you will not have 'periods'.

If you have had the womb and both ovaries removed before the age of fifty you should receive long-term hormone replacement to prevent thinning of the bones. This can easily be provided by your doctor and there is no need to go back to your gynaecologist.

Wendy, who worked as a secretary, was a very pretty girl who had both her ovaries and uterus removed when she was only thirty-two years old. Fortunately she was prescribed HRT straight away and has taken a tablet of oestrogen every day for the past five years. She looks splendid and has no sexual difficulties or medical problems of any kind.

Wendy comes to see me every six months when I check her blood pressure and ask how she is feeling and give her a repeat prescription. I look forward to prescribing hormones for her for at least twenty years or as long as she wishes to take them.

Hormone implants

Hormone implants are sometimes used by gynaecologists to treat women who have had their uterus and ovaries removed. The implant is a small, hard pellet containing either oestrogen and testosterone, or just oestrogen.

You lie flat and the doctor injects a little local anaesthetic into the skin of your abdomen. Then a tiny cut is made and the pellet is inserted through a tube. The tube is removed and the pellet pushed down into the fat under the skin. A stitch or a small plaster closes the opening. Hormones are slowly absorbed from the implant over the course of a year, but if symptoms such as hot flushes recur, it may need renewing after six months.

What are the advantages of an implant?   Implants are used instead of tablets for several reasons. The hormones are more effective because they are absorbed directly into the blood, and are not altered and partly inactivated by having to pass through the gut and liver. There is also less chance of changes in blood clotting, which can occur when hormones are passed through the liver. Then, from your point of view, an implant means there is no need to take tablets every day.

The main disadvantage is the near impossibility of removing an implant if there are side-effects – the doctor would have great difficulty in finding it again.

Oestrogen cream is used to treat vaginal and urethral atrophy after the menopause. It is inserted with an applicator every night for a fortnight, and then one week in four, or as often as required. The lining of the vagina becomes, thick, moist and healthy with this treatment. It is in fact very useful for many problems of vaginal soreness, discharge, or sexual pain in the older woman.

The cream acts in the area where it is applied so a very small dose is often sufficient to keep the vaginal oestrogen level topped up. However, the oestrogen is absorbed into the bloodstream and this may act on the uterus and cause bleeding after the menopause, which would need investigation. Because it is absorbed vaginal oestrogen cream is not safe for women who have breast cancer.

What are the side-effects of HRT?

1. Sometimes women feel sick after taking oestrogen, but this wears off after a couple of weeks.
2. Some people put on weight and get swollen ankles due to fluid retention; this can be treated with diuretic tablets.
3. Hormone preparations containing oestrogen or oestrogen plus progestogen can cause the blood pressure to rise, so you should have a blood pressure check before starting HRT. If your blood pressure is high on several readings it will need observation or treatment. Drugs used to treat high blood pressure can safely be taken with hormone therapy.
4. The breasts may swell and become tender. This often wears off after the first two weeks. If it is a major problem ask your doctor to examine your breasts and then the prescription may be changed to a different HRT preparation.

How long should you remain on HRT?

You can go on taking the tablets as long as you and your doctor are happy about it. There is no need to stop unless you develop one of the following conditions:

1. An illness that is associated with accelerated blood clotting – say, coronary thrombosis or a small stroke.
2. Gall-bladder disease; this is often made worse by hormone treatment and it may be wise to stop it if you develop gallstones.
3. Cancer of the breast, womb or ovary can be made worse by high levels of oestrogen, so if you were unlucky enough to get one of these you would have to stop treatment.
4. Other major diseases such as kidney disease may be made worse by HRT. Your doctor will advise you about this.
5. If you are going to have a big operation, such as a hip replacement, there is an increased risk of blood clotting and the surgeon will prefer you not to take oestrogen for at least a month before the operation. Of course there is no reason why you should not go back on the treatment afterwards.

If you have been taking HRT to prevent hot flushes and you stop very suddenly, the flushes are likely to return. So if you are going to stop taking hormones, try to cut down the dose very slowly, and if possible avoid doing it during the summer or while you are on holiday in a hot climate, as heat makes the flushes worse.

The pros and cons of HRT

As I said at the beginning of this chapter, not everyone is suited to HRT. One of the problems we have faced lately is the enormous expectations women have of it, whatever the chances of its being useful for them, and the possibility of them becoming dependent on hormones. HRT *does not* make you miraculously young, beautiful and slim; and in women over seventy who have not had a hysterectomy it is not a safe or particularly suitable treatment for osteoporosis – women of that age do not want to start 'periods' again. So for them we prescribe anabolic steroids (stanozolol) together with calcium supplements.

Yet there are undoubted benefits for those who are suited, and for them I always recommend HRT. Many women stay on hormone therapy for a long time after the menopause simply because it makes them feel better. It prevents hot flushes and keeps the vagina moist and healthy, so that they can go on enjoying sex without any problems. It stops early thinning of the bones and the indications from research are that widespread use of hormones immediately after the menopause would prevent a lot of the bone fractures that occur in old age. American surveys have shown that women who take long-term HRT are 50 to 60 per cent less likely to suffer fractures of the hip and forearm than those who don't.

The table opposite sums up the main advantages and disadvantages of HRT and will help you decide whether it will be beneficial for you.

HRT if you have a uterus

Advantages	Disadvantages
Cures flushes and sweats	You will have 'periods' while you take HRT
Prevents vaginal dryness	Supervision by doctor is necessary
Prevents osteoporosis	
Cures or prevents ageing changes in vagina and urethra and the 'urethral syndrome'	Endometrial biopsy or D & C is often needed
	Proved risk of uterine cancer unless precautions are taken
	Unknown longterm risk effect on breast and heart
	Expense of regular checks and the endometrial biopsy
	Possible dependency on oestrogen

HRT if you have had a hysterectomy

Advantages	Disadvantages
Cures flushes and sweats	Medical supervision necessary only for heart and blood pressure
Prevents vaginal dryness	
Prevents osteoporosis	Unknown longterm risk effect on breast. Oestrogen alone probably improves cardiac risk unless you have had thrombosis
Cures or prevents ageing changes in vagina and urethra and the 'urethral syndrome'	
	Possible dependency on oestrogen

New findings on HRT

A word on new research before I leave the subject: it is possible that HRT can help serious diseases. A very interesting survey in America found that hysterectomy patients who took oestrogen therapy for up to nineteen years were less at risk from heart disease and cancer. However, the women were financially well off and were compared with women in the general population, who were often poor and of lower social class and had a higher incidence of disease because of this. So it is not yet proved that oestrogens lower mortality – although a later study that compared women from similar backgrounds did show a reduction in deaths from coronary disease in those who had taken oestrogen. This is probably due to the effect of oestrogen in reducing the level of cholesterol in the blood.

Two important surveys are in progress in Britain to try to measure the effect of HRT on patients' death rates, and the incidence of cancer, strokes and coronary disease. It will be some years before the results are available. We do not yet know whether oestrogen combined with progestogen will affect sickness and death rates in a different way from oestrogen used alone.

7 TREATMENT BY THE GYNAECOLOGIST

From what I have said in earlier chapters you will know there are a number of troubles that need investigating by a gynaecologist and some need surgery. These are usually conditions that haven't already been cleared up by treatment your doctor has given you:

- irregular bleeding between periods without an obvious cause (for example, an IUD)
- bleeding more than six months to a year after the menopause
- a late menopause – after the age of fifty-four
- enlargement of the womb, felt as a lump or heaviness in the pelvis
- bad abdominal pain
- a severe vaginal infection or itchiness of the vulva that won't clear up
- difficulty in holding water.

In the UK women who need specialist help are usually sent to a gynaecologist by their doctor. But there are some who feel dissatisfied with their medical care – they may not have been given enough time to explain matters fully to their doctor, or perhaps they feel that the doctor is not sympathetic to their case and they have not been able to communicate properly. If this is so for you, there are two courses of action you can take in the UK. You can ask your family doctor to recommend you to a gynaecologist privately, or you can go to a clinic yourself, where treatment is free. In North America and other countries you can make an appointment with a gynaecologist direct.

The clinics provide an invaluable service. You may make your first appointment over the telephone, and the number of your nearest clinic can be found in the telephone directory or by enquiring at your local hospital or the Community Health Department of your local authority.

There are three types of clinic that deal with menopausal and gynaecological problems. The first is the family planning or contraceptive clinic. This deals with contraception, queries about pregnancy and sexual problems. Clinics for venereal disease, sometimes called Special or Genitourinary Clinics, are the best possible investigators of vaginal discharge (see Chapter 5). They provide careful treatment and follow-up of any pelvic infection. Well Woman clinics, and also cytology or cervical smear clinics, are being set up all over the UK to give advice on gynaecological and sexual problems. All these clinics carry out examinations of the pelvis and cervical

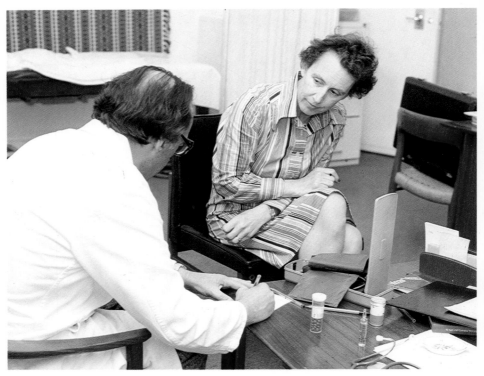

Before you have an operation, make sure your doctor tells you exactly what will be done.

smear tests. A list of clinics in other countries appears at the end of this book.

If you have been examined, either by your doctor or at a clinic, and it is discovered that you need gynaecological treatment, the first thing you should do is to make absolutely sure that you know what is going to happen to you.

Information and consent

A lot of doctors don't perhaps realize how little their patients share their knowledge and confidence about operations. If a patient is upset, she often finds it difficult to discuss treatment in a sensible way and cannot take in information accurately.

> Penelope was an actress separated from her husband. She had two children. When she was nearly forty she developed pain and heavy bleeding. A diagnosis of endometriosis (see Chapter 1) was confirmed by the gynaecologist, who advised her to have a hysterectomy, as she would have 'no further use' for her womb.
>
> Shortly afterwards Penelope came to see me in some distress. She had

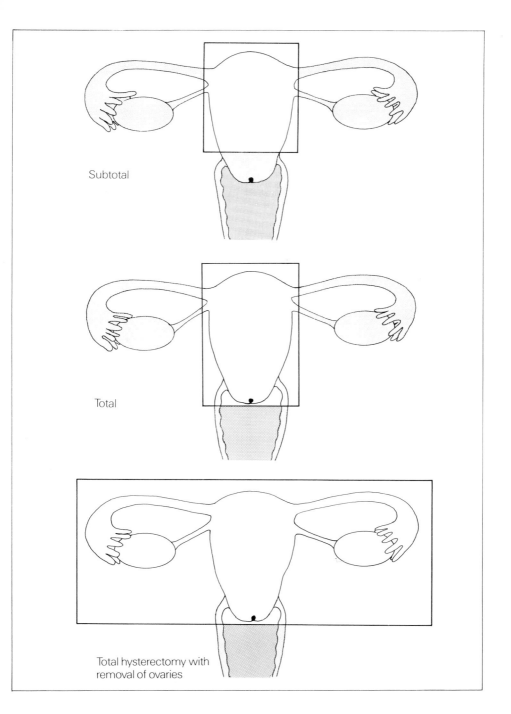

Subtotal

Total

Total hysterectomy with
removal of ovaries

The different types of hysterectomy

found it impossible to explain to the gynaecologist that she was contemplating remarriage and wanted to leave open the chance of another pregnancy. She desperately wanted to avoid having a hysterectomy if possible. I suggested that she might be treated with danazol (see page 16) and the gynaecologist agreed.

Penelope has been examined every few months and the treatment has been very successful in stopping her monthly pain and heavy bleeding.

By discussing her feelings, Penelope avoided an operation she did not want. Nowadays there is a much wider range of treatment available and there may well be an alternative that would suit you better too.

It horrifies me that sometimes people who have had major surgery have hardly any idea of what has happened to them. Don't be afraid to ask – a few minutes spent discussing the situation with your doctor or gynaecologist can save you from this predicament.

Before you have an operation you will have to sign a consent form. First you should know:

- What is being done. Is a part going to be removed?
- Why it is being done. Is it to stop pain or bleeding? To remove a lump? To control fertility? Is there an alternative form of treatment that would suit you better?
- Who will carry out the operation.
- How long you will be in hospital.
- How long you will need to recover.
- How much it is going to cost you. It may be useful to ring up the gynaecologist's secretary to enquire about his fee, the anaesthetist's fee and hospital charges.
- What are the permanent after-effects. Will you be sterile? Will sex be normal?

Some of these questions will be answered for you in this chapter, but it is still important to check everything with your doctor.

D and C (Dilatation and curettage)
This is an examination carried out under a general anaesthetic. It is often arranged for women with heavy or irregular bleeding so that a diagnosis of cancer can be excluded. The D and C itself can cure bleeding after a miscarriage, but it is primarily done for investigation. Similarly, if you have had two cervical smear tests (see Chapter 5) with uncertain findings a D and C may be recommended, as well as investigation of the cervix.

In dilatation the hole in the neck of the womb, the cervix, is dilated, or expanded, until it is wide enough to carry out curettage. A curette, which is either a metal ring on a stem or a tiny spoon, is pushed into the cavity of the womb. Particles are taken from all over the surface of the womb and are sent to the laboratory where they are examined under a microscope.

You will not be sore after a D and C, and can go home the same or the next day. There is no need for any sort of convalescence at home either.

Endometrial biopsy is a similar process to a D and C that can be carried out by an experienced doctor in the consulting room or outpatients' clinic, without an anaesthetic. It is no more painful than having an IUD fitted. A long, blunt nozzle is pushed into the uterine cavity and attached to a syringe that sucks out some of the cells lining the womb.

Hysterectomy

Hysterectomy is the removal of the womb. This operation may be necessary if you have cancer of the womb, fibroids or heavy bleeding. Sometimes hysterectomy is offered to women who menstruate after the age of fifty-five in order to prevent the development of cancer of the womb as it is more common in this group. An incidental advantage to having a hysterectomy is that it is also a contraceptive measure.

> Frances was a forty-year-old Catholic who had troublesome searchings of conscience over whether she should use contraception. She already had four children and she and her husband were only just managing on his small income. She did not feel that she could cope with another baby and she had found that using the so-called 'safe period' approved by the Catholic Church had not prevented two of her pregnancies. Her periods were very heavy and I diagnosed a small fibroid and sent her to a specialist. The gynaecologist recommended a hysterectomy. Frances welcomed this because it would solve both her problems. Her periods would stop and she would have no further risk of pregnancy.
>
> Frances has made a good recovery from the operation and her sex life has improved. The whole family are more relaxed now this cause of anxiety has been removed.

There are four versions of the operation:

1. Subtotal hysterectomy – leaving the cervix in place
2. Total
3. Total hysterectomy with removal of ovaries.
4. Vaginal hysterectomy.

Which operation you have depends on whether you have one of the difficulties I described above, in which case you will have a total hysterectomy – by far the commonest type – or whether you have a cancer that has spread beyond the womb itself, or a disease like endometriosis involving both ovaries and womb. Then you will need the third type. Subtotal hysterectomy is not often carried out these days. Most gynaecologists

After a big operation, let someone else do the heavy carrying for you.

prefer to remove the entire womb so that the risk of cancer of the cervix is eliminated. The womb can be removed 'from below', leaving no visible scar, when a hysterectomy and repair of a prolapse are needed at the same time. This is the fourth operation – vaginal hysterectomy.

There is no point in having your ovaries removed unless they are diseased. As long as one or both continue to function you avoid the symptoms of the menopause, which you will naturally want to put off as long as possible. My advice is do not have hysterectomy with removal of both ovaries unless your specialist is adamant that it is necessary.

Hysterectomy is a very common operation, undergone by 12 per cent of British women at some time during their lives. Over 30 per cent of American women have hysterectomies and the rates in Canada and Australia are similar. The operation is extremely safe, with a recovery rate of 998 women out of every 1000.

The operation – what does it entail?
You will be in hospital for about ten days. A cut is made horizontally along the top of the pubic hair line, and this will leave a slight scar. Your figure will remain normal. If the womb is very large, it may be necessary

to make a vertical cut just to one side of the centre. The scar will soon fade and become inconspicuous. A further internal cut is made at the top of the vagina to release the womb, and a tiny opening is often left in order to drain secretions from the body cavity. You may notice a pale brown discharge for a few weeks after the operation, until this opening closes.

After the operation

- You should be able to return to full-time work after about three months. Light, sedentary work can be started before this.
- You may be asked not to drive for a month, as sudden braking can put a strain on the scar.
- For the same reason you should avoid lifting heavy weights for at least three months.
- Sex can be resumed after six weeks, but you may be rather dry, so it is a good idea to use a lubricant at first until your natural lubrication has improved. You will of course no longer need to use contraceptives.
- If hysterectomy has been recommended for a condition such as heavy bleeding or fibroids, you will soon feel much better after the operation than before and be able to take part in any physical activity you have always enjoyed.

The 'artificial menopause'

After hysterectomy many women continue to experience cyclical changes and feel bloated every month. The retained fluid is lost by passing a lot of urine. This pattern is not surprising as the monthly changes in mood and body weight are under the control of the ovaries and pituitary gland, which have not been removed.

Although hysterectomy without removal of the ovaries should not lead to a deficiency in hormone production, about 20 to 30 per cent of women do complain of hot flushes afterwards. This may be caused by temporary deficiency in the blood supply to the ovaries and usually gets better without treatment.

If your ovaries are left behind they should go on secreting oestrogen until the time of the true menopause around the age of fifty, when you will probably experience some flushes. You can have hormone therapy at this stage, but it is not usually necessary immediately after the operation.

Will you feel depressed?

Anyone having a hysterectomy for fibroids or heavy bleeding will feel so much better that depression is unlikely. If, though, you have had the operation for a more general complaint such as lower back pain or sexual difficulty, you may feel depressed soon after the operation. Your trouble can itself be a cause, and the operation may trigger another attack.

Do seek support from those around you, especially your partner; if this does not seem to be a solution for you, talk to your doctor about your condition.

Many women feel that they would like to have more counselling and support before and after the operation; busy outpatient clinics have not much time for this, although sometimes medical workers provide an individual service. The Hysterectomy Support Group has been set up in the UK to help women who feel anxious and would like more information. The address of this organization is given in the Useful Addresses section at the end of the book.

Removal of an ovary
One or both ovaries can be removed if they are diseased or if you have cysts there. The operation will leave a small abdominal scar as if you had had a sterilization by tubal ligation (see Chapter 2), but you will have no side-effects if only one ovary is removed.

As with a hysterectomy the scar will take about a week to heal and you will have to take things very gently at first to allow it to knit properly. You will certainly feel tired for a while because of the changes brought about in your hormone balance.

If both ovaries are removed, a sudden menopause is experienced. You will probably feel a bit low and have hot flushes. To cope with these, follow the advice I give on page 20. But if they continue to be a nuisance, talk to your doctor about them. Unless you are suffering from a disease that rules out hormone treatment, HRT can be extremely effective in clearing them up (see Chapter 6).

Often both ovaries are stopped from functioning as part of the treatment of breast cancer. This can be upsetting as the symptoms of the menopause are added to the worry about cancer and perhaps a mastectomy. Don't forget that this treatment is a life saver for a significant number of years, so it is certainly worth going in for if it's recommended.

During the months after treatment a woman will need a great deal of sympathy from family and friends and advice and support from the doctor, and often trained counsellors can be of extra help. In this case hormone treatment would not be advisable, but the doctor may offer lubricants to aid sex, and anti-depressant tablets. It is very important to ask for help and to involve close friends and relatives, as it makes the way to recovery so much easier.

Colporrhapy
A prolapse of the womb is very common – about 20 per cent of our patients have some prolapse (see Chapter 5). This often causes problems with bladder control: either you feel that you have to pass urine very suddenly (urge incontinence) making it difficult to walk about freely, or you pass small quantities when you cough or sneeze (stress incontinence). To diagnose the complaint, an X-ray film can be taken of the way the bladder

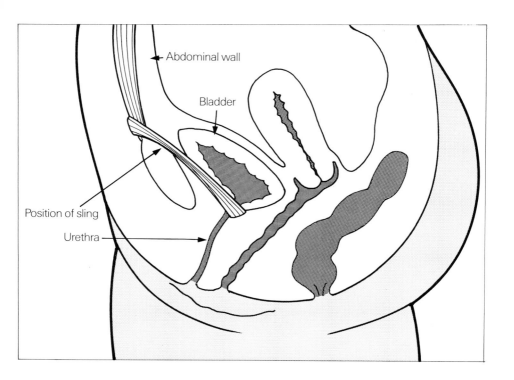

Abdominal wall

Bladder

Position of sling

Urethra

One type of colporrhapy, which will put right a prolapse.

empties. This will show the looseness of the supporting muscles or lack of coordination in muscle action.

Urge incontinence can be simply treated with a course of exercises designed to retrain the bladder (see page 71). It is often helped by using oestrogen cream as well to thicken the walls of the urethra and vagina and help them to resist infection.

Stress incontinence is treated by colporrhapy, an operation that tightens the supports under the neck of the bladder and removes the slack tissue of the vagina. Sometimes a sling of tissue from the abdominal wall is used to hitch up the base of the bladder and support the urethra. The Manchester Repair is a similar operation that also involves the removal of the cervix.

After the operation You may have difficulty in passing urine for a few days. To help, you may be fitted with a catheter, a soft tube that passes from the bladder through the urethra to the outside. Until it is removed, you will probably be given antibiotics to prevent infection.

Once you return home you will need to take life gently for two or three months, avoiding lifting heavy weights or going in for violent exercise, but in other ways you will feel perfectly all right and there will be no soreness.

Pat was forty-eight when she noticed that 'something was coming down in her vagina'. She had trouble with holding her water especially when she coughed or ran for a bus. She had two children and they had both been large babies, involving a difficult delivery. When I examined her she had a prolapse, the front wall of the vagina and base of the bladder bulging into the vaginal cavity. This got bigger when she coughed or strained.

Pat consulted a gynaecologist who carried out a neat operation, removing the bulge and tightening the supports of the bladder and womb. She was in hospital over a week and when she returned home she had to be extremely careful not to lift heavy weights for three months. This took some arranging. Pat's mother had to come over to cook meals and do the shopping. But it was all worthwhile; she has no problems now. Sex is fine and she can go out for the day without wearing a pad for protection. She says she has felt much more confident about her social life since the operation.

8 QUESTIONS AND ANSWERS

I hope that reading this book has explained all you want to know about the menopause. But there are many small though sometimes worrying details people ask me and in this chapter I would like to answer as many of those as space allows.

How long will my menopause last?
The menopause itself is merely the date of the last menstrual period. However, you may experience flushes and irregular periods for a few years beforehand. After the menopause flushes occur more frequently for about two years and then disappear. Some women have mild symptoms from their early forties until around the age of sixty.

Will I follow the same pattern as my mother or sister?
No, not necessarily. Menstrual patterns have changed during the past thirty years and it is common for women to have a later menopause than their mothers.

If I get flushes, will they be worse during the day or at night?
Flushes are often worse at night and may interfere with sleeping. Most women find that they flush more easily if they get tense or 'uptight' and of course embarrassment may bring a blush to your cheeks which can then turn into a prolonged attack of flushes. Drinking alcohol or coffee in the evening is often the trigger for late night flushes.

If I have one menopausal symptom badly, will the others also be bad?
There is no reason why you should get all the menopausal symptoms badly, if one symptom is severe – unless you have had your ovaries removed. A sudden artificial menopause may cause bad flushes, depression and loss of interest in sex and the same woman can have problems with vaginal soreness and osteoporosis later on. However, all these problems respond to treatment with hormones and unless there is a definite medical reason why you should not be given HRT you should ask your doctor for it.

Will a dowager's hump certainly develop and if so when shall I begin to notice it?
There are a few women who inherit a family pattern of early deformity of

the spine but this is unusual. If you do not have a strong family history there is no reason why you should not have a straight back until over the age of seventy-five. Keep your back straight, sit and walk tall, eat the right food and stay active in the fresh air as long as you possibly can. The little old ladies with bent backs in our practice are mostly those who have been sitting indoors for many years.

Do people who've suffered premenstrual tension necessarily have a bad menopause?

No. The two conditions are quite separate and distinct. But women who suffer from depressions and tension or have insecure, stressful marriages may have premenstrual tension, and it is not surprising that this group of women are also likely to suffer from depression and neurotic symptoms during the pre-menopause.

Will I be tired and irritable during the change?

The peak age for tiredness, moodiness and depression is just about two years before the menopause. These symptoms often clear up when the periods stop and flushes start to appear. Most women of any age feel a bit jaded if they are coping with a job, a family and social life as well. Do try to 'mother' yourself as there is often no one else who will advise you to relax, cut the corners on the housework, and make sure that you have your share of food, fun and freedom.

Shall I have bad headaches?

Headache is not a symptom of the menopause. A large population study of middle-aged men and women showed that both sexes suffered frequently from headache and there was no increase in women around the time of the menopause.

How will my sleep be affected?

You are likely to sleep less well as you grow older. This is an effect of age and has nothing to do with the menopause. You probably need less, so that your individual sleeping time shortens from eight to seven or six hours. This is normal and nothing to worry about and happens in both sexes. Hot flushes often interfere with sleep unless you do something about them like using cotton sheets (not a duvet) and keeping the room cool. Hormone treatment is very effective and is more useful than sleeping tablets if you are being woken up by hot flushes and sweats. If your main problem is one of waking very early in the morning and perhaps feeling dreadful, you may be suffering from depression. It is important to get medical help as this condition is eminently treatable and is not something that you can 'snap out of' yourself.

How long shall I go on enjoying sex?

As long as you want. Many older women and men admit to feeling sexy and having intercourse until the late seventies. The commonest reason for stopping is the lack of a partner. Don't be put off by the puritanism of young people – they will feel differently about it when they are your age! If you or your partner are experiencing physical difficulties just go and see your doctor to make sure that you have all the help you need. Although you may feel that you do not want to make unnecessary demands your husband may be flattered at having a wife who appreciates him. Arousal may be slower and you could find that hand stimulation is necessary to start an erection. Take things gradually and do not be afraid of trying a different position, perhaps lying on your side. Lubricant jelly is a tremendous help in easing penetration. It will probably be easy for your partner to delay ejaculation as older men are good at this. As long as your partner can get an erection and intercourse does not hurt you you should be able to enjoy sex for many years after the menopause.

If one of you doesn't enjoy and doesn't want to have sex although the other is willing, then you should decide whether your love is strong enough to make you want to change the situation. Help is available from interested doctors and psycho-sexual therapists if you feel that it is worthwhile. Many couples opt for companionship and friendliness rather than passion, and if one of you becomes ill this may force the issue. Try to keep the lines of communication open between you so that you are each aware of what the other wants – no easy matter at any age.

If I stop taking the Pill, what is the safest contraception?

You may use the mini-Pill, or a barrier method like the sheath (condom) or the cap. Alternatively you and your partner may decide that sterilization offers the most complete protection, now that you have completed your family. If you take the combined type of HRT, this will cause you to have 'periods'. Although you will not become fertile because of this, HRT does not protect you against pregnancy. So you should use a barrier method until the age of fifty-five.

Is the 'safe period' a useful method of contraception just before the menopause?

The safe period (rhythm method) depends on timing your sex life in such a way that intercourse only takes place at the time in each month when you are infertile, that is just after menstruation and in the week before the next period. The couple keep a record of the previous menstrual periods to estimate the probable limits of cycle length and calculate the safe period from this. A thermometer is sometimes used to decide whether a woman has ovulated, as this is accompanied by a rise in body temperature. Even if a couple have used this method successfully until their forties, it is hardly ever safe during the pre-menopause. There are enormous variations in the

93

length of cycles at this time, from very short (about eighteen days) to very long (several months). There is often shortening of the post-ovulatory phase of the cycle so that a couple using the temperature method may find that as soon as they decide that it is safe to have intercourse menstruation intervenes. It is not uncommon to find that a woman who has used this method successfully when her periods were regular becomes pregnant in her mid-forties.

Is there a danger of cancer from HRT?

The risk of cancer of the endometrium (see page 17) is increased between four and eight times if a woman with a womb uses oestrogen-only HRT. If you have had a hysterectomy then this side-effect cannot occur, but we still do not know whether there may be an increased risk of breast cancer.

Supplemented HRT – the kind containing oestrogen and progestogen – prevents cancer of the womb developing if progestogen is given regularly for at least ten days every cycle. It may be a good idea to have the lining of the womb checked at the start of therapy and at two-yearly intervals.

Smoking cigarettes increases the risk of many types of cancer and it is a good idea to stop or cut down your smoking.

If you take oestrogen and continue having 'periods' are you still fertile?

No. When you have stopped ovulating and having periods you have reached the menopause and this is not reversible. The 'periods' which you experience with combined HRT are artificial withdrawal bleeds produced when you stop taking progestogen at the end of each cycle.

If I take HRT, how long should I continue?

Gynaecologists are not agreed about the answer to this question. Some suggest that you should take it in the smallest dose for the shortest possible time. Other doctors arrange for very long-term treatment, say fifteen to twenty years, although they are not always able to ensure that their patients continue to take it. My own view is that women can go on taking HRT as long as they and their doctor are happy about it and provided that they have long-term supervision. This means being positively vetted at the start of therapy, so that women who have a dangerous condition which would be made worse by the treatment are not prescribed HRT. A woman should contact her doctor when she needs repeat prescriptions so that he or she can enquire about her health. She needs blood pressure checks and examination of the womb at least yearly, and may need a two-yearly endometrial biopsy. She needs to feel her breasts every month. The argument for really long-term treatment is the prevention of thinning of the bones and fractures in old age.

Look forward with pleasure to the new opportunities in the coming years.

Will I get menopausal symptoms when I stop HRT?

Yes, you will probably suffer from flushes if you reduce the dose suddenly. You have become mildly dependent on the drug and changes in body chemistry have occurred which prevent you temporarily from making use of your own natural oestrogens. Just cut down the dosage gradually and if possible arrange to come off the pills during cool weather. Your 'rebound' flushes are harmless and will get better. You will soon (in about three months) be able to make use of your own natural supply of oestrogens.

My partner has had a prostate operation. How will this affect our sex life?

Men are usually as potent after the operation as they were previously, i.e., they are able to have an erection if they could do so before the operation. Sometimes they have problems over ejaculation as the seminal fluid is less in quantity and may be missing altogether (it is diverted up into the bladder). Lubrication could also be diminished so you may need to use an artificial lubricant. Do not worry if sex is dry – you can have satisfactory intercourse without emission. Many surgeons tie the vas deferens on each side and of course if this is done it will mean that your partner is sterilized.

My partner seems to have lost interest in sex. Is this because of me being menopausal?

No. Not unless you have discouraged him because of feeling off-colour or having a painful dry vagina – read the book to find out what you can do about these problems. You need to ask yourself whether everything is all right between you. Is the relationship a happy one? If not, then you will need to ask why things have gone wrong and try to put them right – sometimes a relationship has been deteriorating for many years and the menopause is just a convenient label to stick on an unhappy situation. If you are fond of one another but he doesn't want sex, could he be suffering from depression, either a depressive illness or a reaction to strains at work, illness or fear of redundancy? The question you have asked is itself a hopeful sign that you have decided to take stock of the situation and want to do something about it.

Why do some women have no symptoms and others such severe ones?

A large population of women who live in the Netherlands were studied to find out which types of women had the worst symptoms. It showed that career women suffered less than housewives, but those with a monotonous, badly paid job had most problems at the menopause. So your life situation affects your symptoms. Other research suggests that the thin fair woman is more likely to have severe flushes and, later, osteoporosis than an overweight, heavily built woman. So the type of person that you are will affect whether you have symptoms. On the whole it is best to aim at a stimulating life and staying as fit as possible – this keeps your adrenal glands in working order so that they manufacture plenty of natural hormones.

I have thickened around the waist, although I'm not eating more than before. Is this due to the menopause?

Yes and no. The change in the balance of hormones has some effect on your figure. Before the menopause oestrogen predominates over the male hormones (androgens) and this favours large breasts and hips and a smallish waist. After the menopause oestrogen levels fall and this frees more androgen so that you tend to have a thicker waist, smaller breasts and a deeper voice. At the same time, the rate at which you burn up calories is reduced as you grow older, so that although you have not changed your diet you have some energy left over which is stored in the form of fat. You may have to cut your calorie intake in order to stay the same size.

How can I avoid having tightness of the vagina?

Try to keep up your sexual activity as long as possible. You may need to use a lubricant and if this does not help you may need oestrogen cream from your doctor. Use the cream every night for a fortnight and then about seven nights a month, or even just occasionally.

What help can I get from a menopause clinic, and will I need a letter from my doctor to go to one?

A menopause clinic is usually situated in the out-patient department of a teaching hospital. You should take a letter from your own doctor to explain what problems and treatment you are having. The gynaecologist will listen to your story and examine you. A speculum is used to examine the cervix and take a cervical smear. He may carry out an endometrial biopsy (see page 85). The nurse will check your height, weight and blood pressure and analyse your urine. Blood tests are often carried out to see if you are anaemic or suffering from thyroid disease, and also to check the level of hormones in the blood. The doctor should be able to let you know whether your symptoms are due to the menopause and if you can be helped by treatment with hormones. He or she will arrange for you to have any treatment which is necessary and may be in touch with your family doctor over future supervision.

Do Well Woman clinics help women with menopausal troubles?

Well Woman clinics are very helpful to women with menopausal troubles. Not all the women who attend there have this kind of problem and the clinic staff usually take care to give the sort of individual help which each woman really needs. They arrange blood pressure readings and cervical smears, for example, but would not impose this kind of test on anyone who felt unwilling to have it. The most important aspect of the clinics is their leisured approach to history-taking and counselling. They allow lots of time for you to unburden yourself and tell them all your problems, including social and financial matters, but do not put any pressure on women to have a particular treatment.

USEFUL ADDRESSES

UNITED KINGDOM
There are twenty-one menopause clinics in Great Britain at present. They all require women to be referred by a doctor, usually their general practitioner. Here are addresses for the main centres; your doctor should tell you which your nearest clinic is:

Chelsea Hospital for Women
Dovehouse Street
London SW3 6LT

Glasgow Royal Infirmary
Castle Street
Glasgow G4 0SF

The John Radcliffe Hospital
Oxford

King's College Hospital
Denmark Hill
London SE5 9RS

Manchester General Hospital
Crumpsall
Manchester M8 6RB

Peterborough and District Hospital
Thorpe Road
Peterborough

Royal Hallamshire Hospital
Glossop Road
Sheffield S10 2JF

Royal Infirmary
39 Chalmers Street
Edinburgh EH3 9ER

Simbec Research Centre
Merthyr Tydfil
Wales

Women's Hospital
Gynaecological Clinic
Catherine Street
Liverpool

Women's Hospital
Leeds

Wythenshawe Hospital
Southmoor Road
Manchester 22

IRELAND:
Coombe Hospital
Dublin 8

Samaritan Hospital
Lisburn Road
Belfast

A great deal of help on menopausal problems may be obtained from Well Woman, Cytology, or Family Planning Clinics. These clinics may be listed in your telephone directory or can be found by asking at your local hospital or Department of Community Health. You do not need to be referred by your doctor.

Counselling Services:
Well Woman Clinic
Wood House
Park Clinic
Wythenshawe
Manchester

Women's Health Concern
16 Seymour Street
London W1H 5WB

FPA clinics providing fee-paying menopause advice and treatment:

Sheffield FPA Clinic
17 North Church Street
Sheffield

West Midlands FPA Clinic
7 York Road
Birmingham B16 9HX

Pregnancy:
'Who cares for the problem pregnancy?'
Lifeline Pregnancy Care
268 High Street
Uxbridge
Middlesex

Support groups:

Judy Vaughan
Hysterectomy Support Group
Rivendell
Warren Way
Lower Heswall
Wirral L10 9HV

Women's Health Information Centre
Ufton Community Centre
12 Ufton Road
London N1

Endometriosis Society
65 Holmdene Avenue
Herne Hill
London SE24 9LD

There is a Northern Ireland contact for exchanging names and addresses. She is Rosemary Morrison, 161 Logan Walk, Old Warren, Lisburn, Co Antrim.

SPoD (Sexual Problems of the Disabled)
The Diorama
14 Peto Place
London NW1 4DT

UNITED STATES

The majority of women seeking help with menopausal problems are able to obtain this from their gynaecologist or their family physician so the need for special menopause clinics is not so pressing as in some other countries. However there is a private menopause program called **Mid-Life Challenge**. Information from:

Marcha P. Flint
Department of Anthropology
Montclair State College
Upper Montclair
New Jersey 07043

Other useful addresses:

American Endometriosis Association
Health Center
Wisconsin

The Counselling and Psychotherapy Center
100 27th Street
Fairlawn
New Jersey 07410

CANADA

A Mature Women's clinic has been set up in the Department of Obstetrics and Gynaecology of Toronto General Hospital and provides care either on a doctor-referred or self-referral basis. Other useful addresses:

Canadian Fertility Society
2065 Alexandre de Seve
Suite 409
Montreal, PQ
H2L 2LW

College of Family Physicians of Canada
4000 Leslie Street
Willowdale, ON
M2K 2R9

L'Institut International du Stress
659 Hilton Street
Montreal, PQ
H2X 1W6

Migraine Foundation
390 Brunswick Street
Toronto, ON
M5R 2Z4

Society of Obstetricians and Gynecologists of Canada
14 Prince Arthur Avenue
Suite 109
Toronto, ON
M5R 1A9

Women's College Hospital
76 Grenville Street
Toronto, ON
M5S 1B2

Women's Health Education Network
PO Box 1276
Truro
Nova Scotia
B2N 5N2

AUSTRALIA

Dr Lorraine Dennerstein is currently conducting a Menstruation-Menopause Clinic at the Queen Victoria Medical Centre. Women are usually sent by their doctors but many come because they have heard of the clinic:

University of Melbourne
Department of Psychiatry
Clinical Sciences Block
c/o PO Royal Melbourne Hospital
Victoria 3050

A menopause clinic has been established at:

The Royal Hospital for Women
Paddington
NSW

There are others in each capital city and a few in community health centres. Many of these only accept women sent by their general practitioners.

Family planning advice from:

Australian Federation of Family Planning Associations,
70 George Street
Sydney
NSW 2000

INTERNATIONAL DRUG NAMES

Generic Name	United Kingdom Trade Name	Canada Trade Name
calcium lactate gluconate	Sandocal	Calcium-Sandoz Forte
conjugated oestrogens	Premarin	Premarin; Oestrilin
conjugated oestrogens + norgestrel	Prempak-C	Enovid-E
danazol	Danol	Cyclomen
depot progestogen (medroxyprogesterone)	Depo-Provera	Depo-Provera
dydrogesterone	Duphaston	not available
ethinyl oestradiol	available as tablets	Estinyl
ethinyl oestradiol + methyltestosterone	Mixogen	Climacteron (injection)
medroxyprogestrone	Provera	Provera
mestranol + norethisterone	Menophase	Program
metronidazole	Flagyl	Flagyl; Neo-Tric
norethisterone	Primolut N; Utovlan	Norlutate
nystatin	Nystan	Mycostatin; Nilstat
oestradiol	Progynova; Hormonin*	Estrace
oestradiol + levonorgestrel	Cyclo-Progynova	Ovulen 0.5
oestriol	Ovestin	not available
oestrogen-progestogen	Ovran; Eugynon 50; many others	Ovral
piperazine oestrone	Harmogen	Ogen
quinestradol	Pentovis	not available
spermicidal jelly	Ortho-Gynol; Duragel; Staycept	Ortho-Gynol

*The product contains active ingredients other than that in the generic name column.

	United States	Australia
Generic Name	**Trade Name**	**Trade Name**
calcium lactate gluconate	not available	Sandocal
conjugated oestrogens	Premarin	Premarin
conjugated oestrogens + norgestrel	not available	not available
danazol	Danocrine	Danocrine
depot progestogen (medroxyprogesterone)	Depo-Provera	Depo-Provera
dydrogesterone	not available	Duphaston
ethinyl oestradiol	Estinyl	Estigyn
ethinyl oestradiol + methyltestosterone	Estratest	Mixogen; Primodian
medroxyprogesterone	Provera; Amen	Provera
mestranol + norethisterone	not available	not available
metronidazole	Flagyl	Flagyl; Trichozole
norethisterone	Aygestin; Norlutate	Primolut N
nystatin	Mycostatin; Nilstat	Mycostatin; Nilstat
oestradiol	Estrace	Progynova
oestradiol + levonorgestrel	not available	Ovestin
oestriol	not available	Ovestin
oestrogen-progestogen	Ovral; Nordette	Ovral; Eugynon
piperazine oestrone	Ogen	Ogen
quinestradol	not available	not available
spermicidal jelly	Ortho-Gynol; Gynol 11; Conceptrol	Ortho-Gynol

ACKNOWLEDGEMENTS

For their help with the preparation of this book I would like to thank:

Mr R. Butler Manuel, Dr Anthony Clift, Dr Lorraine Dennerstein, Prof Max Elstein, Mrs Pat Entwistle, Dr Fleur Fisher, Mrs Jean Robinson and Dr Julian Tudor Hart.

I would also like to thank Linda Sonntag and Mary Banks for editing and supervising the layout of the manuscript.

1984   JEAN COOPE

The publishers are grateful to the following:

For permission to reproduce photographs: Bavaria-Verlag, Munich (page 47); Jan Kuczerawy, NSW Australia (page 42); Miller Services, Toronto (page 38); Pictor International, London (page 86); Picturepoint, London (page 51); Rex Features, London (page 82); and Zefa, London (page 53).

The cover and photographs on pages 19, 20, 27, 46 and 95 were modelled by Marie Cecilia Martin; photography by Roland Kemp. The photograph on page 20 was taken at the Bathroom and Shower Centre, London.

The diagrams were drawn by David Gifford, and the information for the calcium table on page 59 is based on McCance and Widdowson's *The Composition of Foods* (HMSO).

Finally, thanks are due to Jennifer Eaton, BSc, MSc, MPS, for information on international drug name equivalents.

INDEX

Page numbers in *italic* refer to the illustrations.

Other books in the
Positive Health Guide series

ENJOY SEX IN THE MIDDLE YEARS
Published in association with the National Marriage Guidance Council
Dr Christine Sandford

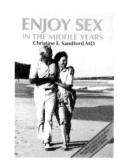

Sex in the middle years should be fun, easy, trouble-free. But ageing physically and the stresses of family and work can affect your relationship and the quality of your love-life. Dr Christine Sandford, a marriage guidance counsellor with many years' experience of dealing with sexual problems, explains the roots of your problems and gives sympathetic, practical advice on how to tackle them.

THE HIGH-FIBRE COOKBOOK
Recipes for Good Health
Pamela Westland
Introduction by Dr Denis Burkit

Although most people now realize the enormous importance of eating high-fibre food to help avoid many of the commonest Western ailments, few know how to put this knowledge into practice in a varied and interesting way. Here at last is a book that combines the healthy benefits of high-fibre eating with good imaginative home cooking.

GET A BETTER NIGHT'S SLEEP
Prof Ian Oswald and Dr Kirstine Adam

For the millions of insomniacs, these world-renowned sleep experts help to break the vicious circle of anxiety over lost sleep leading to more restless nights. They offer practical, scientifically based advice on the best ways to avoid sleeplessness and wake refreshed each morning.

THE BACK – RELIEF FROM PAIN

Patterns of back pain – how to deal with and avoid them

Dr Alan Stoddard

BEAT HEART DISEASE!

A cardiologist explains how you can help your heart and enjoy a healthier life

Prof Risteard Mulcahy

DON'T FORGET FIBRE IN YOUR DIET

To help avoid many of our commonest diseases

Dr Denis Burkitt

ASTHMA AND HAY FEVER

How to relieve wheezing and sneezing

Dr Allan Knight

OVERCOMING ARTHRITIS

A guide to coping with stiff or aching joints

Dr Frank Dudley Hart

PSORIASIS

A guide to one of the commonest skin diseases

Prof Ronald Marks

DIABETES

A practical new guide to healthy living

Dr Jim Anderson

HIGH BLOOD PRESSURE

What it means for you, and how to control it

Dr Eoin O'Brien and
Prof Kevin O'Malley

THE DIABETICS' DIET BOOK

A new high-fibre eating programme

Dr Jim Mann and the Oxford Dietetic Group

STRESS AND RELAXATION

Self-help ways to cope with stress and relieve nervous tension, ulcers, insomnia, migraine and high blood pressure

Jane Madders

VARICOSE VEINS

How they are treated, and what you can do to help

Prof Harold Ellis

ECZEMA AND DERMATITIS

How to cope with inflamed skin

Prof Rona MacKie

ANXIETY AND DEPRESSION

A practical guide to recovery

Prof Robert Priest

ACNE

Advice on clearing your skin

Prof Ronald Marks

OVERCOMING DYSLEXIA

A straightforward guide for families and teachers

Dr Bevé Hornsby

EYES

Their problems and treatments

Michael Glasspool, FRCS

CONQUERING PAIN

How to overcome the discomfort of arthritis, backache, migraine, heart disease, childbirth, period pains and many other common conditions

Dr Sampson Lipton